The ITV book of
THE OLYMPICS

ITV BOOKS

First published 1980

Independent Television Books,
247 Tottenham Court Road,
London W1P 0AU.

Photographs

Black and white

Page

4 Popperfoto (top right); Allsport (centre right); Colorsport (bottom centre)
5 Associated Press (top right); Colorsport (centre, bottom right)
8 Colorsport
9 Colorsport
12 John Topham (top right); Central Press (centre right); Popperfoto (bottom left); Colorsport (bottom right)
22 Popperfoto (top left, centre right, bottom left); Central Press (bottom right)
25 John Topham (top centre, bottom left); Popperfoto (centre right); Allsport (bottom centre)
37 Allsport (top left, top right, centre right);
55 Allsport (top, bottom centre)
59 Popperfoto (top right, bottom left); Melbourne Herald (bottom right)
60 Popperfoto (bottom right)
67 Popperfoto (top left, bottom left, centre right)
83 Popperfoto (top, bottom)
86 Popperfoto (top right, centre left, bottom left); Associated Press (top left)
95 Allsport (top right); Popperfoto (centre left); Associated Press (bottom left)
107 Allsport (top left, centre right); Popperfoto (centre left, bottom right)
108 Colorsport (bottom right)
138 Colorsport (top left, bottom left, right); Allsport (centre)
139 Colorsport (top left); Allsport (bottom left, centre, right)
140 Allsport (top left, centre, top right, bottom right)

Colour photographs

Page

6 Wolfgang Nordwig (E. Germany) pole vault gold, 1976.
18 Alberto Juantorena (Cuba), 400m and 800m golds, 1976.
31 Valery Borzov (USSR) 100m and 200m gold, 1972.
47 Don Quarrie (Jamaica) 200m gold, 1976.
68 Kayak singles event, Munich 1972.
76 Wilma Rudolph (USA), 3 sprint golds, 1960.
96 Olga Korbut (USSR) star of 1972 gymnastics.
101 John Akii-Bua (Uganda) 400m hurdles gold, 1972.
113 Epee gold medalist Fenyvesi (Hungary) faces Jung (W. Germany) 1972.
121 Alexeev (USSR) superheavyweight gold 1976.
133 Peters (GB) pentathlon gold, 1972, with West Germany's Rosendahl (silver) and East Germany's Pollack (bronze).
141 Gunther Nickel (W. Germany) hurdler, 1976.

Cover

Centre: C. Barkovsky (USSR); left: Rita Schmidt (GDR); right: D. Bedford (GB). Photos by Allsport.

Allsport: pages 11, 18, 31, 47, 52, 60, 68, 76, 96, 101, 108, 113, 121, 124, 133, 141.
Popperfoto: page 6
John Topham: page 26
E. D. Lacey: page 38
Gerry Cranham: page 89

Contributors

James Coote Until 1979 he was the much respected Athletics Correspondent of the *Daily Telegraph*, London. He began this book, but tragically was killed in an air crash before it was completed.

Bob Trevor Co-founder, with Jim Coote, of the British Athletics Writers Association. For 10 years he was Athletics Correspondent for the London *Evening News*, and is now Sports Editor for the BBC World Service. He took over the major part of this book on the death of Jim Coote.

Sam Leitch Controller of Sport and Outside Broadcasts at Thames Television, London, and joint Executive Producer of Independent Television's Moscow programming.

Eric Lahmy One of Europe's best known swimming writers, who reports for the French sporting daily newspaper, *L'Equipe*.

Richard David Sports statistician, whose wide experience includes work on the *Guinness Book of Records*.

Robert Bressy Illustrator with an international reputation for his sports work for publishers throughout Europe.

Hardback: ISBN 0-900727-70-5
Paperback: ISBN 0-900727-69-1

Origination by ReproSharp, London EC1
Printed in Italy.

The ITV book of THE OLYMPICS

James Coote
Bob Trevor
Sam Leitch
Eric Lahmy
Richard David
Robert Bressy

ITV BOOKS

Contents

The 1936 flame leaves Olympia.

Jesse Owens (USA) 1936.

Bob Seagran (USA) 1972.

Nadia Comaneci (Rumania) 1976.

Kriss (USSR) and Hoskyns (GB) 1964.

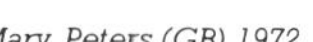

Mary Peters (GB) 1972.

1980 Moscow: The world will be watching

Half the world will watch the Moscow Olympics on television. Two hundred and fifty electronic colour cameras will be zooming in on the most choreographed games of all time for a colossal audience of two thousand million viewers.

Compare this with Wembley and the cloudy 1948 Olympics. Nine cameras servicing 80,000 sets within a fifty-mile radius of Alexandra Palace. Such is the march of television time.

ITV will mount its biggest and most expensive TV sports operation from the heart of the Soviet capital next July and August.

Biggest coverage yet

From Studio 14 in the new Olympic TV Centre at Ostankino about 150 hours of Olympic action will be recorded and transmitted to ITV viewers. Dickie Davies, Brian Moore and the rest will be virtually living in the studio, which is just half an hour's taxi ride from the Kremlin.

The TV centre is brand new. There are 20 studios using 20 TV channels, which means twenty different programmes for the various parts of the world. Montreal in 1976 had 16 channels, Munich in 1972 used 12 and Mexico City in 1968 had seven.

So the Soviets, encircled by satellites and knee-deep in electronic gear, have legislated for the show-it-again-and-again spectacular. No sports event in history will have endured so much scrutiny.

The Moscow planning has been thorough, but a balance between the clinical facts and human factors has been maintained.

The star bear

For instance, Misha the Moscow mascot, has been introduced to the world of the five Olympic rings. Or to be more formal, Mikhail Potapych Toptygin, a good-natured but pigeon-toed bear cub, chosen by Soviet viewers as the symbol of the 22nd Olympiad in preference to a hare, an otter, a chipmunk and a wood grouse.

Misha will be to Moscow what Paloma the pigeon was to the Mexicans, what Waldi the daschund was to the West Germans and what the Canadian beaver of just four years ago was to Montreal.

In Russia, bears have a star status. They can ride bikes, play soccer, skate, box and dance. They are merry, inquisitive and strong.

This quaint attention by the Olympic planners to both the electronic wizardry and cartoon fun will once again make the action (mostly from Moscow, but also using the cities of Leningrad, Tallinn, Kiev and Minsk) an irresistible attraction for British viewers.

The Olympic Games have not risen to stardom overnight. The mass audience has built up over the years. London (1948) had the first live TV action, but the audience was small. Helsinki (1952) and Melbourne (1956) went backwards, with film instead of electronic coverage.

Rome (1960) saw the European Broadcasting Union's debut. CBS of America thrilled their viewers with a new hero, an 18 year-old light heavyweight boxer called Clay.

Tokyo (1964) used the Early Bird satellite and bounced pictures to 39 countries. The world began to get a taste for the games and the Japanese produced the first-ever live colour pictures for their own viewers.

Mexico City (1968) produced a colourful games and records galore fell at these high altitude Olympics. British viewers saw their first live TV colour. The rights cost 10 million US dollars.

Valery Borzov the top Soviet sprinter of 1972 and 1976 will appear in Moscow.

1980 Moscow: TV audience of 1,500 million

Outside the Lenin Stadium, site of the 1980 games.

Munich (1972) the fee jumped to 15 million dollars. Over 100 hours of television appeared on British screens. It was a triumph for the BBC who had wisely invested in a Munich-based operation. They were right on the spot for exclusive pictures of the infamous Israeli massacre.

Munich also saw the birth of gymnastics as a major Olympic sport, thanks to Olga Korbut. This tiny Russian girl mesmerised one thousand million viewers.

Montreal (1976). A super TV deal was made by ABC of America. They paid 25 million dollars for the rights. Then they sold 85 million dollars' worth of advertising during their Olympic air time.

These games were seen through more than 100 electronic colour cameras and the world audience jumped to 1,500 million.

Now to the fourth successive Olympic capital beginning with the letter M — Moscow (1980) with 3,000 sports journalists, 400 photographers, 100 film cameramen, 800 TV and radio broadcasters and 3,000 TV and radio producers, cameramen and technicians. The television rights are still selling. They could be as high as 130 million dollars.

Soviets think big

Why the attraction? No other event in sport appeals to so many families of all colours and creeds. Moscow will be full of rituals and records. The Soviets are obsessively anxious to make this the greatest of all the modern Olympics.

As *Time* magazine reported: 'The Soviets are approaching the challenge much the same way as the pharaohs went about building the pyramids, with single-minded intensity and a cast of thousands.'

This time we can expect huge television audiences. It does not take much for the British to switch on by the million to live international sport. Our love affair with little Olga and her pigtails produced 16 million British viewers per night for gymnastics in 1972.

The generally-accepted record Olympic audience for the United Kingdom is the twenty million BBC viewers who were glued to the Brendan Foster 10,000m final from Montreal.

NBC of America will transmit 152 hours in the USA to an estimated 170 million viewers. They have paid out over 100 million dollars for the rights and coverage.

European Union

ITV and BBC will be part of the powerful European Broadcasting Union complex, which will be sending out two live programmes daily. In addition to this, four of the leading European broadcasting organisations will mount their own exclusive programmes from Moscow. These are ITV, BBC and the two West German channels, ARD and ZDF.

As well as NBC and the four Europeans, other world broadcasters, like Asahi of Japan, Channel 7 from Australia and CBC of Canada will shape their own programmes from Moscow.

I have been privileged to be part of the detailed planning for the ITV Moscow operation. John Bromley of London Weekend Television and I are joint Executive Producers for the Olympics just as we were for the 1978 World Cup.

ITV will take around 100 people to Moscow — commentators, reporters, engineers, producers, vision-mixers and an assortment of technical staff. We would have liked to take 50 more, but Olympic accreditation is as tight as Kremlin security.

We will work with Moscow television colleagues. We will have our own offices, studios, control rooms, video tape recorders. We will take live pictures from the various Olympic venues, talk to our commentators around Moscow and talk to London — but not at the same time, we hope!

Talent from all companies

The personnel will be drawn from the ITV companies specialising in international sports production. It will be very much a Network operation, paid for by all the companies.

We will call on Olympic performers from past games to provide expertise from the commentary position — track stars like Adrian Metcalfe and Alan Pascoe and swimming gold medallist David Wilkie.

Commentating for the young

We will keep in touch with the youth of the country by taking teenager Barbara Slater to Moscow as the ITV gymnastics' expert. She is a former British champion and has been working for the past year with the sports production staff of both Thames and London Weekend Television.

Naturally in this very competitive age of television ITV and BBC are likely to be locked into their own Olympic confrontation in the corridors of Ostankino, so it would not do for me to reveal all the ITV plans.

But from the start ITV's thinking about Moscow '80 has been to add something new to TV journalism, a dimension which will take us into the eighties in style. We cannot afford to forget our huge family audience.

Nothing on my ten working visits to Moscow in the past three years has impressed me quite so much as the vast new TV set-up, created by the Russians.

1980 Moscow: Media men of East and West

Ten years ago the 14-storey Ostankino building was completed with its 28 TV studios, 70 radio stations and 190 videotape recording machines. A huge mass of glass, wires and 18,000 technical staff it stands in the shadow of the Ostankino TV tower. Over 500 metres tall this is the supreme landmark of the skyline of Moscow which is long in history but short of skyscrapers.

To this building has now been added a new, five-storey television complex, directly across the road. With 20 more TV studios and 100 more radio stations, it is the most concentrated TV headquarters in the world.

Four communication satellites and two landlines will take the Olympic action into Europe.

Quite the most impressive TV executive I have met in Moscow with a key role at the games is Alexandre Ivanitsky, Merited Master of Sport, and head of Moscow TV and Radio sport.

He is 6ft 3ins, weighs fifteen stones, loves mushroom picking as a weekend holiday break and won a gold medal at the Tokyo Olympics as a freestyle wrestler.

Today he is widely respected throughout the TV world as a brilliant planner and careful thinker about new ways of projecting sport on the small screen. He is a mild swallower of 'tonic and gin' (as he calls it) and his massive handshakes leave knuckles with a fragile hangover.

Stars behind the screen

Planning and planners are the keynote of this operation. Some of the men responsible for the pictures coming your way next summer never hit the headlines, and will never be seen in front of the cameras. But their skill and patience are admirable. Men like Bill Ward, OBE. He heads the European Broadcasting Union's Operations Group in Moscow, a terrifying responsibility. Bill lives in the West Country, was a TV cameraman for the BBC at Alexandra Palace, and produced many of the early *Sunday Night at the Palladium* shows for ATV before becoming their Programme Director. He also headed the EBU team at the World Cup in Argentina.

Alan Chivers is a TV Olympic veteran who holds a key executive role in Moscow for the EBU. He was the BBC producer at the 1948 Olympics in London and was the producer in charge of the 1966 World Cup from the same stadium.

Communication engineers are the most important men during the four years it takes to plan a TV Olympics operation.

Norman Taylor is the Chief Engineer at the BBC. He has made so many trips to Moscow that it's whispered Ivanitsky and his mates have issued Norman with a Red Rover flying ticket!

Roger Philcox from London Weekend Television is ITV's top communication wizard for Moscow. His job is to get the pictures from the Russian sporting venues into the TV centre in Moscow and out again to London, and make sure the sound is alright as well.

A new Moscow for the games

Moscow has certainly changed in the three years I have been popping in and out of the Ukraine, Roussea, Berlin, Sovietskaya and National hotels.

It used to take two hours between landing at Moscow's Sheremetyevo airport and receiving your baggage through customs. Now there is a new terminal. Two more airports will be ready for the Games.

The capital in July and August faces the biggest onslaught of Western visitors since a non-athletic gent called Napoleon arrived in Moscow in 1812.

There will be 300,000 Western visitors in Moscow for the three weeks of the games. That's more than half the total Moscow usually hosts in one year. Hotel capacity will be 80,000. In 1976 it was 50,000. A new, glittering, 28-storey hotel called the Cosmos has just been completed. It cost £90 million and is French-owned.

More than 1,000 French and Yugoslav workers spent three years building this new flagship of the Intourist hotel fleet. It has de luxe suites at £100 per night, seven restaurants, an Olympic-size indoor swimming pool and is within a ten-minute walk of the new TV centre. The Cosmos is our telly digs for the games.

Tired taxis to the rescue?

Taxis are torture in Moscow. I once sent my wife on an errand from the Sovietskaya hotel to the TV centre and then on to the Bolshoi Ballet.

She had to mime her way there. First the hands for the TV screen and then a ten-minute mini version of Swan Lake before she completed the journey.

So I am delighted to be able to report that 5,000 Moscow taxi drivers are being sent to night school for lessons in English, French, Spanish and German.

Instructor Ludmila Bychinova can be heard daily at Taxi Garage No 11 in Gorki Street saying things like 'Good day, Mr Smith, let me put your things in the trunk.'

I wish everyone well in the Moscow cabs. There are 16,000 of them. They are old. They smell of petrol. Most of them have lost their springs, and they roar around Moscow's 1,500 streets.

The inside of the Lenin Statium has been refurbished for 1980.

1980 Moscow: Russian prestige at stake

The 300,000 foreign visitors to the games will not be the only ones in the Soviet capital. There will be another 300,000 from the rest of Russia, 12,000 athletes and officials, 3,500 judges, 3,500 participants in sports congresses, plus those few media folk I mentioned earlier — to say nothing of Moscow's eight million inhabitants!

How much are the games costing the Soviet Union? Unofficial estimates put construction costs at around £200 millions. Which is less than half the total for Montreal. A total of 99 Olympic construction projects have been undertaken. But there are fewer new stadiums and buildings than for the 1976 or 1972 Olympics.

Valery Borzov, one of the Russian's greatest home-ground hopes.

Any seat better than none

Most Soviet sports complexes are hard on the bottom and the bladder. But I am told there will be an urgent improvement in the ladies' facilities at the newly-renovated Lenin Stadium in Moscow. One room was provided for 10,000 spectators, and this is in the main stadium for the games.

The Lenin Stadium is the showpiece of the Luzhniki sports complex, which is the site of seven Olympic events, the track-and-field athletics, soccer, gymnastics, volleyball, judo, water polo and the individual Grand Prix equestrian event on the last day of the games.

The complex runs next to the glorious Lenin Hills where young Moscow brides come along and drink a toast on their wedding days.

Old and new buildings

Although the Lenin Stadium is 23 years old it has been extensively spruced up and is a perfect venue for the Olympic showpieces. It is 20 minutes drive from the centre of the city and of course the site of the opening and closing ceremonies.

The indoor stadium of the Olympiiski Sports complex will have a seating capacity of 45,000, the largest covered sports stadium in Europe. Swimming, boxing and basketball are the sports to be held in this, the most central of all the venues.

The rowing canal in the Moscow suburb of Krylatskoe is also Europe's best. There will be seats for 21,000 and boathouses for 600 craft.

The equestrian complex will be at the Bitsea Wood Lane Park with 12,000 seats and stables for 450 horses.

The Velodrome Krylatskoe is one of the dazzling eye-openers. A nationally-organised architectural competition decided its design. It has room for 6,000, while the Druzhba (Friendship) Hall is set on diamond-shaped exterior struts that make it look like a crab. It will house 3,000 spectators and the volleyball events.

In the south-west of Moscow the Olympic Village is the biggest and best ever constructed — eighteen massive blocks of flats, each 16 storeys high, covering an area of 270 acres. This will be the headquarters for the 12,000 competitors and coaches.

There will be a 10,000 volume library on the premises, a disco, two cinemas and a concert hall. The Bolshoi will perform there. But beer cellars (in Montreal style) are out.

Russian hopes and heroes

What of the Soviet sporting heroes themselves at the games? Vasily Alexeev, the world's strongest man, will be chasing gold medals, which he won at the Munich and Montreal Olympics. The Soviet Union has 300,000 weightlifters and 1,000 specially-equipped gymnasiums serve the country's pride-and-joy sport, dating back to the Russian folk heroes.

Vasily is an engineer who has broken 80 world records. He is 38 in 1980, captain of the Soviet weightlifting squad, a man with huge shoulders and astonishingly black and bushy eyebrows.

Yelena Belova is another Merited Master of Sport. She won gold medals in the individual foil and her trio of passions are fencing, history and bibliography. Her fourth Olympics are coming up.

Valery Borzov is a rarity indeed. Few sprinters have ever competed at three Olympics. Valery now tries to do what no sprinter has ever done — win medals at all three games.

He won two gold at Munich and two bronze in Montreal. He will be in the Soviet sprint relay team. And if they win what joy for this handsome runner who is now married to one of the most beautiful and successful of Soviet sportswomen, Ludmilla Tourischeva, former world and Olympic champion gymnast.

So much for the plans, the cameras, the heroes, the brand new complexes and the Moscow Olympic revolution which is under way.

What is the event which almost 30 million British viewers will be waiting and hoping for? The sight of Messrs Coe and Ovett challenging each other for gold and silver respectively in the classic track middle distance events. Why they might even make it a dead heat!

Sam Leitch

Right: Daley Thompson, top British decathlete for 1980.

Below left: Sebastian Coe (GB), contender for the 1,500m in Moscow.

Right: Tessa Sanderson (GB) faces strong competition in the javelin in Moscow.

Top: The stadium in Athens where the first games of the modern era and the so-called interim games of 1906 were held.

Right: The opening of the 1936 games, charged with political overtones, visible as the audience makes the Hitler salute.

Bottom left: Equestrian accident during the three day event in Stockholm in 1956. Because of Australian quarantine rules the riding was held in Sweden instead of Australia.

Bottom right: The most amazing medal collector in the history of the Olympics. Mark Spitz on his way to his seventh gold in Munich, 1972.

The ancient Greek Olympic Games

The date 776BC marks the beginning of an era in Greek civilisation. In that year the first recorded Olympic Games took place.

We know this because a citizen of Elis, named Korebos, is recorded as the first Olympic winner. His victory was an unusually peaceful affair. No feat of arms was mentioned in the text. Indeed, one of the most remarkable things about the Greek games was the compulsory truce imposed on all participants for the duration.

For the early Olympics were not simply athletic contests. They were religious festivals, exalting the culture of body and mind. As a result their origins are an uncertain mixture of myth, and facts provided by archaeologists. The stadium at Olympia has been excavated, complete with starting line.

Once begun, the games developed along lines familiar to us today. The programme expanded, as did the prestige of victory, and with it controversy about professionalism and even cheating. Winners were heroes and one was even crowned king.

In the end it was the religious aspect of the games which hastened their end. Christianity became the official religion of the Roman Empire, and all pagan festivals, the Olympics included, were stopped.

The ancient games: from legend to a race programme

The origins of the ancient Olympics are lost in legend. Some stories say that Zeus began them to celebrate victory over his father Kronos, by which he bacame king of the gods. Later Hercules re-established them. Others say that Pelops began the games after his successful campaign against the King of Pisa. And that King Iphitus took up the tradition to put an end to the plague raging in the Peloponese.

The Hellenic games

However, of some things we are certain. Athletic contests were only open to the people of Hellas, not a country as Greece is today, but rather a community of people with like cultural traditions, as Christendom was in the middle ages, or as Islam still is today.

These Greeks valued competition and made physical excellence part of their religious observance. Some of the first races were between local boys eager for the privilege of lighting the priest's sacrificial flame.

There were other games besides those at Olympia — the Pythian games were dedicated to Apollo at Delphi, the Nemean games to Zeus at Nemea and the Isthmian games to Poseidon at Corinth.

The first known winner

The first games were simple foot races 200m long. The first known winner of this event was Koreobos, a citizen of Elis, in 776BC. In 724BC a race was run over 300m and in 720BC another over 4,800m. These races made up the entire Olympic programme for more than a century. It was only later that new events were added, including chariot racing and wrestling.

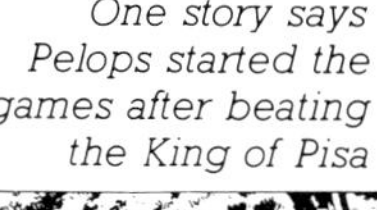

One story says Pelops started the games after beating the King of Pisa

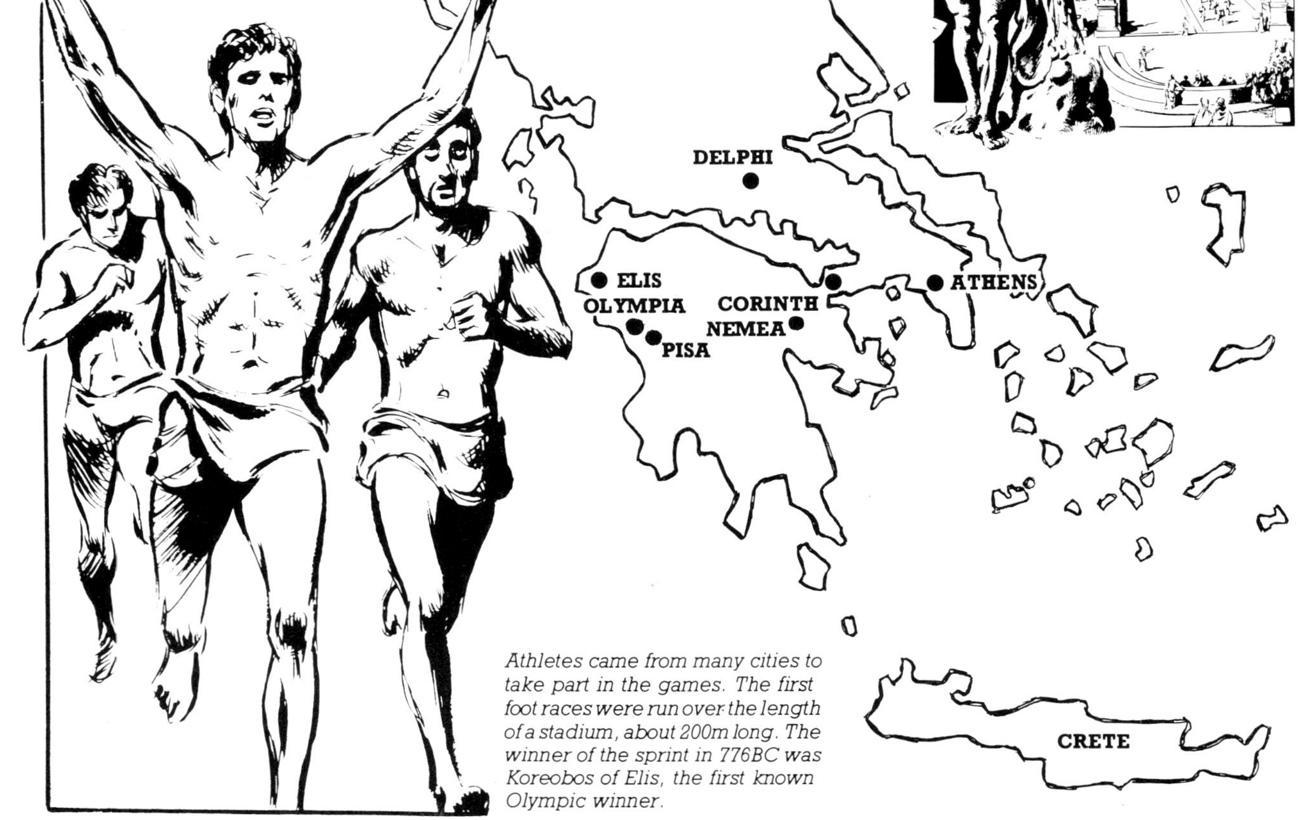

Athletes came from many cities to take part in the games. The first foot races were run over the length of a stadium, about 200m long. The winner of the sprint in 776BC was Koreobos of Elis, the first known Olympic winner.

The ancient games: Popular festival at Olympia

In the ancient world, state and cultural affairs were inextricably mixed up with religion. So naturally religious ceremonies occupied a large part of the five days allowed for the games. They included offerings to Zeus, to whom the site of Olympia was sacred, including the sacrifice of 100 cattle on the third day of each games.

Athletes, artists, intellectuals

The games attracted enormous crowds. People came not only for the athletic contests and the religious ceremonies, but also for the artistic presentations. Artists produced special works for the Olympics. One of these was Pheidias' statue of Zeus in gold and ivory, which was considered one of the seven wonders of the ancient world. Later, the great Greek intellectuals, like Socrates and Plato, attended the games. Philosophical debates took place in public.

The Olympic truce

This great popular festival was facilitated by the Olympic truce. For three months peace was observed among the warring states of Greece, so that the Olympics could take place. The truce never stopped any of the wars, but it did allow people to gather from all over the country. Later on, when Greece became part of the Roman Empire, Pax Romana made the truce unnecessary.

Congestion at Olympia

When the great crowds assembled at Olympia, the conditions under which they lived were atrocious. There was no sanitation, no water, but lots of heat, noise, dust and flies.

There is a story of a slave who, having disobeyed his master, was sent to Olympia as a punishment!

The Olympics were popular festivals as well as athletics matches. Artists contributed sculpture. Philosophers held debates.

The games were originally religious celebrations, including sacrifices to ancient gods.

Socrates and Plato, famous Greek philosophers, also came to the games.

The site of Olympia was sacred to Zeus, king of the gods. Thousands attended the ceremonies.

The ancient games: Heroes in epic events

The first Olympics consisted entirely of foot races, 200m or one length of the stadium, 400m and 4,800m. But gradually new events were included: the pentathlon in 708BC, then wrestling and boxing, followed by chariot racing in 680BC, then horse races, the pancratium, and even armed soldiers' races.

Spectacular chariot races

The chariot race soon became the most important event of the games. It was held on the second day, and as an epic it surpassed everything imagined by Hollywood film producers. In 462BC a record number of 41 chariots lined up at the start. Of these only one completed the five and a half mile course over 12 laps of the hippodrome. Immediately afterwards, on the same debris-strewn course, the bareback riding race took place.

Battles of brute force

The pentathlon was held on the second day and the three running races on the fifth and final morning. The afternoon was set aside for the contact sports — boxing, wrestling and the pancratium. These were tough battles of brute force, with few rules, no time limits, no ring and no weight categories.

The greatest champion of the ancient Olympics was without doubt Milo of Croton, who won the wrestling six times between 540 and 516BC. He also won six times in the Pythian games, nine times in the Nemean games and ten times in the Isthmian games, before retiring unbeaten.

The best runner was Leonides of Rhodes who in two Olympics won all three foot races — the 200m, 400m and 4,800m – all held on the same morning. As for Theagenes of Thassos, in one year he carried off the boxing and pancratium prizes in all the Olympic, Isthmian and Pythian games.

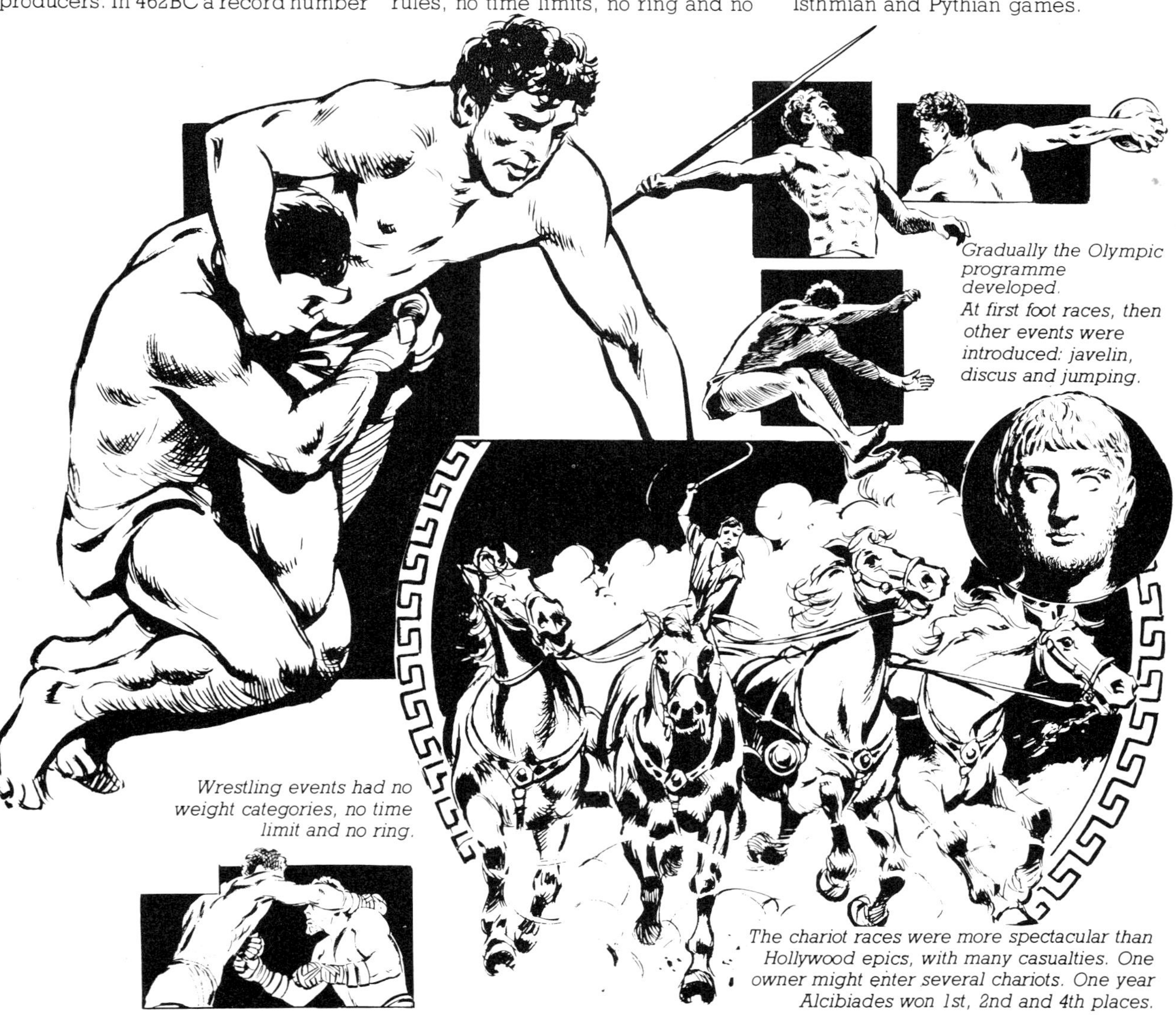

Gradually the Olympic programme developed. At first foot races, then other events were introduced: javelin, discus and jumping.

Wrestling events had no weight categories, no time limit and no ring.

The chariot races were more spectacular than Hollywood epics, with many casualties. One owner might enter several chariots. One year Alcibiades won 1st, 2nd and 4th places.

The ancient games: Decadence and decline

Glory was the main reward of Olympic victors, but it certainly was not the only one. Winners were well rewarded by their home towns. One city even introduced a system of athletic scholarships in the sixth century BC. And in 300BC Ephesus was awarding prizes of silver for various events.

Amateurs and professionals

The spirit of amateurism, so dear to the modern Olympic movement, did not exist. Professionals and amateurs took part on an equal footing. The organisers of some games offered valuable prizes to attract athletes of quality in quantity. But the organisers of the Olympics refused any such idea: the standing of the games was sufficient to maintain their supremacy.

Corruption and prestige

With enormous sums of money in circulation at games in many cities, there was inevitably corruption. Athletes frequently fixed the race in advance and shared the prizes later. But in general the games at Olympia seem to have avoided the worst of such practices and this of course further enhanced their prestige, which reached such a pinnacle that one town in Asia Minor offered 30,000 drachmas (one hundred times a legionnaire's annual pay) to have an Olympic victor take part in their local games.

Even if Olympic athletes were not paid they became valuable properties, like today's footballers. They were received home with a Triumph, a sort of municipal parade. Some were even given pensions that they could pass on to their children.

Christianity brings the end

Strangely enough it was not the corruption of the games that brought about their demise. It was their continuing religious significance. Christianity had conquered the Roman Empire. All pagan festivals, like the Olympic games, were banned by decree of the Christian Emperor, Theodosius I, in 393AD.

The prestige, and sometimes the rewards of a champion were spectacular. One boxing victor became King of Armenia. Some states offered athletic scholarships and huge prizes.

With such glory and riches at stake, corruption was widespread. The Romans continued the idea of games, but not in the Olympic spirit.

103
217
450

Coubertin and the modern revival

Pierre de Fredi, Baron de Coubertin, was almost unrecognised in his own time for his achievement of founding the modern Olympic Games. For the first several Olympiads his name was not even mentioned by French newspapers.

Coubertin was something of a crank, obsessed by the sporting inadequacy of the French education system, and determined to reform it. He travelled widely, spent his personal fortune and wrecked his health, studying and preaching the virtues of sport. He failed to reform French education, but he did manage to revive the Olympic Games.

There had been various local attempts, in Germany and in England, to stage athletic contests, some of which were grandly called 'Olympic'. And Britain, Coubertin discovered, already possessed an amateur sporting ethic in its public schools.

But it was the Frenchman, with his single-minded determination, who first suggested establishing the games in the spirit and form we know them today. In spite of strong opposition, his proposals were eventually accepted by the French Athletic Association in November 1892. With the present Olympics so popular, it is hard to appreciate how difficult he found it to gain acceptance for his idea.

The rebirth of the Olympic Games

The modern Olympic movement owes its origins to the vision and perseverence of one man, Pierre Fredy, Baron de Coubertin. This small, frail Frenchman, born in 1863 to a rich and influential family, had one passionate interest in life — sport. He practised gymnastics, rowing, riding and to the surprise of contemporary Parisians, training runs in the park. He was convinced that sports were essential to the well-being of every individual and even society at large. The revived Olympic Games would he hoped, be the perfect vehicle for the promotion of his ideas.

Thomas Arnold's example

He despaired of the French education system's neglect of sport and returned for inspiration to Britain's Rugby School and its Headmaster Thomas Arnold of *Tom Brown's Schooldays* fame. The rigorous Victorian public schools, he thought, 'prepared one for the world better' than the 'mediocre Napoleonic system'. 'Sport must be practised with fervour, even with violence', he wrote.

In 1890 Coubertin visited the Shropshire village of Much Wenlock, which a Dr Brooke had made into a famous sporting centre by establishing the Much Wenlock Olympian Society. He travelled to other parts of the world, Germany, Sweden, America and found a growing interest in educational sport. This, he felt, could be welded together into an international movement.

Coubertin misunderstood

At home he was completely misunderstood, when in 1892 he proposed to an athletics conference the re-establishment of the Olympic Games. Some thought he was suggesting a theatrical reconstruction in period costume. Others thought the athletes would compete naked, or that the games were for Frenchmen only. To his dying day in 1937, Coubertin remained unappreciated in France. According to one biographer, he was 'one of the few Frenchmen left undecorated'.

But eventually he began to assemble a considerable following from all over the world. In Paris in 1894, 79 delegates from 12 countries attended the International Congress for the re-establishment of the Olympic Games. It was unanimously decided to hold the first modern games in Athens two years later.

Some early attempts, like the Cotswold Olympics started in 1636, tried to revive the idea of the games, but it took the drive of Pierre Fredy, Baron de Coubertin, to create the modern Olympics. He was a passionate enthusiast for many sports.

Coubertin's ideas were received sceptically, but in 1894 he assembled an international conference in Paris and there it was agreed to start the modern Olympics.

1896 Athens: Opposition from the Greek government

The Greek delegation at the Paris conference was wildly enthusiastic at the prospect of the revived Olympics. Mr Bikilas, the Greek representative, became chairman of the new International Olympic Committee. It was decided that although the games were to be held every four years, as in ancient times, the first modern Olympics would be held only two years ahead, in 1896.

Princes and millionaires

The prime minister of Greece was not so enthusiastic. The government of Mr Tricoupis was in no position to accept any financial responsibility for the games. Athens declined the honour of staging the event. Coubertin rushed to Greece. He found a royal patron in Prince Constantine, the heir to the throne, and the grandfather of Crown Prince Constantine, a gold medalist in sailing in 1960. The Prince agreed to chair the Hellenic Olympic Committee and contributions were solicited in Greece and abroad. The response was splendid. A millionaire businessman, Mr Averoff, contributed one million drachmas towards the rebuilding of the Olympic stadium in marble. Mr Tricoupis was soon obliged to resign.

Thirteen nations take part

Meanwhile Coubertin was trying to persuade as many nations as possible to participate. In the end 13 agreed to attend: Australia, Austria, Britain, Bulgaria, Chile, Denmark, France, Germany, Hungary, Sweden, Switzerland, The United States and Greece. Most athletes made their way to Athens at their own expense.

The Olympic Anthem

On 5 April 1896, King George of Greece opened the games before a crowd of 60,000 people. Prince Constantine delivered a speech and the composer Spyros Samaras conducted an imposing performance of his Olympic Anthem, with massed choirs and bands. His anthem has since become the official hymn of the Olympic movement.

The Athens games were threatened before they even began by the opposition of the Greek government, unable to contribute financially. Coubertin went to Athens and engaged the support of the Crown Prince and many rich Greeks, whose contributions helped rebuild the stadium.

The Greek government refused to help as it was almost bankrupt.

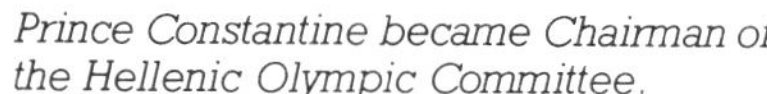

Prince Constantine became Chairman of the Hellenic Olympic Committee.

On April 5 1896, the games opened with a crowd of 60,000 present.

Top left: Percy Hodge (GB) winning the 1920 3,000m steeplechase.

Centre right: Jack Lovelock (NZ) breaking the world record and winning the 1936 1,500m.

Bottom left: Paavo Nurmi (Finland) ahead of Duquesne (France) at the finish of the 1928 3,000m steeplechase.

Bottom right: Harold Abrahams (GB) winner of the 1924 100m. He is still the only Briton to win this event.

1896 Athens: US takes first Olympic honours

The first modern Olympic winner was an American called James Connolly. He was a talented man and he knew it. His teachers at Harvard, where he was studying, opposed his trip to Athens. But the man who later became a doctor, a journalist and a Pulitzer Prize winner didn't let that discourage him. After taking the triple jump title with a distance of 13.71m (44ft 11¾ins), he telegraphed his family back home: 'The Greeks have conquered Europe; I have conquered the world.'

Novel way to start

Another American, the sprinter Burke, astonished everyone with his novel, crouching start. It helped him to win both the 100m and 400m, although in neither case was his time very fast. The Athens track was in a dreadful condition and in the 400m he could manage only 54.2sec, against his American 440yd record of 48.6sec.

Instruction from a statue

The discus was an event which the Greeks were determined to win. The famous Myron statue, the Discus Thrower, was studied for hints on technique. Greek competitors trained long and hard. But all this was to no avail against the beginner's luck, or inspiration, of the American Garrett, captain of Princeton.

He had never thrown a discus before in his life, but his distance of 29.15m (95ft 7¾ins) was unbeatable, and a national disaster for Greece. Paraskevopoulos and Versis had to be content with second and third places. Garrett also came first in the shot, second in the long jump and third in the high jump.

There were other events besides athletics — shooting, fencing and gymnastics were included, as well as swimming, which was held in the sea near the port of Piraeus. The water was so cold that the American champion Hoyt leaped out again immediately after diving in. Sailing and rowing events were cancelled because of bad weather.

Dancers for a harem

Following the ancient Greek tradition, various artistic events appeared on the Olympic programme. There were stage shows, concerts and performances by the ballet company of the Paris Opera. The French President, Felix Faure, was there to present the dancers to the Shah of Persia, who apparently wanted to purchase the entire corps de ballet for his harem!

James Connolly (USA) won the triple jump and the first Olympic title of the modern era.

American sprinter Burke astonished everyone with his strange starting technique.

The discus was an event the Greeks wanted to win, but the American Garrett took the title, in spite of a careful study of classical sculpture by the local athletes.

The Shah of Persia attended the games and is reputed to have wanted to take the entire Paris Opera Corps de Ballet into his harem.

1896 Athens: From Phidippides to Spyros Louis

For the Greeks the most important event was the marathon. In 490BC the Athenians inflicted a crushing defeat on the Persians at Marathon, some 25 miles (40km) from Athens. According to legend a soldier called Phidippides ran all the way from the battlefield to the city to announce the victory, only to die of exhaustion on arrival.

Two thousand three hundred and eighty six years later a French philologist, Michel Breal, offered Coubertin a silver cup for the winner of a race from Marathon to Athens. Since then the marathon has been part of every Olympic games, although it is only since 1908 that the distance of 26 miles 385yds (42.195km) has been standardised.

National pride at stake

The Greeks considered the race a matter of national pride. Of the 16 runners who took part, only four were not Greek. The contestants spent the night before the race in Marathon. Among them was the unknown Spyros Louis, from the village of Amaroussion, near Athens, who is reputed to have spent the night fasting and praying in front of his icons.

Foreigners drop out

The start was at 2pm, in the heat of a sizzling afternoon. The foreigners led to start with, but dropped out one by one. Last to go was Flack of Australia, who gave up at 37km. Kellner of Hungary did manage to finish the race, but he was almost 10 minutes behind the winner, Louis. The local hero was feted at the finish. Crown Princes George and Constantine hoisted him onto their shoulders.

The international games

It was a fitting climax to the games. The Olympics had been launched successfully. And the Greeks felt, somewhat naturally, that in future as in the past, all Olympics should be held on Greek soil.

In spite of the King's determination to retain the games for his country, Coubertin was adamant. He had conceived the Olympic games as a truly international event. They could not belong to any country in particular. A different city must have the honour of staging them each time. His plan has been upheld to this day.

In 490BC the Athenians defeated the Persians at Marathon. A soldier called Phidippides ran the 25 miles to Athens with the news, but died of exhaustion on arrival. The legend was commemorated in 1896 with a race which is still in the Olympic programme.

The Greeks considered it a matter of national pride to win the first modern marathon race. Spyros Louis prayed for victory and achieved it, to be congratulated by Crown Princes George and Constantine.

Top: The Olympic Committee which organised the 1896 games, with Baron Pierre de Coubertin second from the left.

Bottom left: Spyros Louis, winner of the 1896 marathon.

Centre right: Gymnasts performing at the Athens stadium built for the 1896 games.

Bottom centre: The first gold medal of the modern era.

Top: Start of the men's 100m in Athens, 1896. America's Burke astonished everyone with his new crouching start.

Left: Raush of Germany was the only non-American swimmer at the 1904 games.

Above: The Swedish team at the opening of the 1912 Olympics.

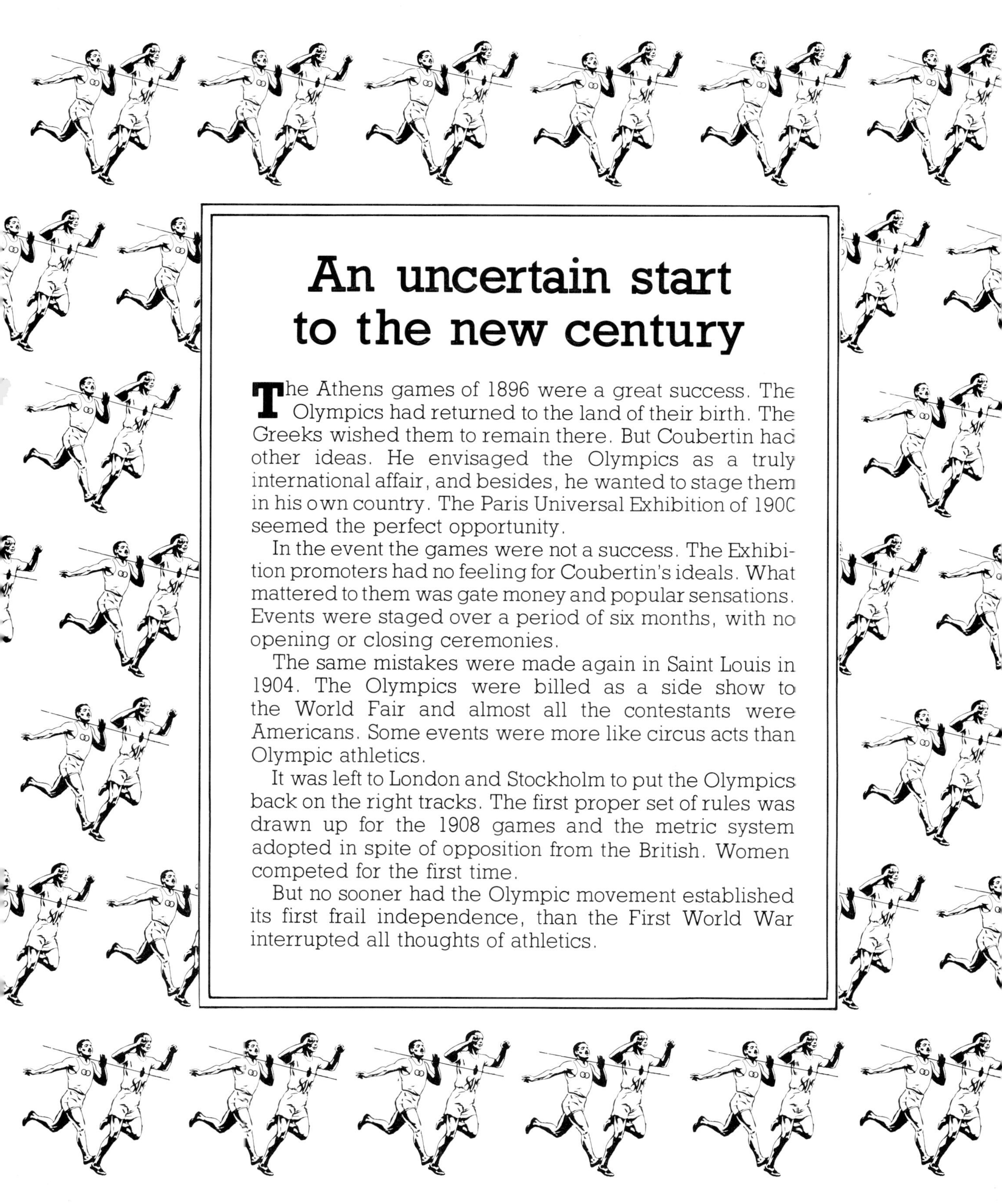

An uncertain start to the new century

The Athens games of 1896 were a great success. The Olympics had returned to the land of their birth. The Greeks wished them to remain there. But Coubertin had other ideas. He envisaged the Olympics as a truly international affair, and besides, he wanted to stage them in his own country. The Paris Universal Exhibition of 1900 seemed the perfect opportunity.

In the event the games were not a success. The Exhibition promoters had no feeling for Coubertin's ideals. What mattered to them was gate money and popular sensations. Events were staged over a period of six months, with no opening or closing ceremonies.

The same mistakes were made again in Saint Louis in 1904. The Olympics were billed as a side show to the World Fair and almost all the contestants were Americans. Some events were more like circus acts than Olympic athletics.

It was left to London and Stockholm to put the Olympics back on the right tracks. The first proper set of rules was drawn up for the 1908 games and the metric system adopted in spite of opposition from the British. Women competed for the first time.

But no sooner had the Olympic movement established its first frail independence, than the First World War interrupted all thoughts of athletics.

1900 Paris: Overshadowed by the Great Exhibition

Coubertin's ideal of staging the Olympics in a different place every four years was to cost him dearly. By comparison with the spectacular success of Athens, the Paris Olympics of 1900 were a disaster, and the following Olympics in St. Louis, USA, even worse.

Slick sensationalism

The founder of the games thought that, as Paris was staging the Great International Exhibition in 1900, the Olympics would be assured of support from both the public and the fair organisers. He was disappointed. Coubertin's amateurs were a source of amusement and derision, while the slick sensationalism of the fair monopolised the public attention.

Forty-eight million people passed the turnstiles of the exhibition. The Olympic athletic events achieved a maximum audience of 3,000.

The athletics went off better than the rest of the Olympic programme. They were held at Croix-Catelan, west of the city, between July 14 and 22. Once again the Americans proved themselves the master athletes, taking 17 of 22 possible titles.

Irving Baxter, an American Indian, astonished everyone with his high jumping technique. He dived over the bar forwards, landing on his hands and won with a height of 1.90m (6ft 2¾ins).

Flanagan (USA) won the hammer with a throw of 51.23m (16ft 1in) — so far that he almost hit some spectators.

The marathon was won by a Frenchman, Michel Theato, a gardener from the Paris race course, who accepted money for competing. He ran the race in under three hours in temperatures of more than 32 deg C (90 deg F) in the shade, but was not awarded his gold medal until 12 years later!

On the rough grass track, Britain's Charles Bennett demolished the 1,500m world record with a time of 4min 6.2sec. Another British runner, Tysoe, won the 800m in a time of 2mins 01.2sec.

British tennis monopoly

The British achievements were not confined to the track. Jarvis won the 1,500m freestyle swimming. In cycling Johnson won the kilometre against the clock. And in tennis Doharty won the men's singles, Cooper the ladies' singles, while both the men's and mixed doubles were won by British players.

The Great Exhibition in Paris was a huge commercial success which completely overshadowed the Olympics.

Irving Baxter (USA) astonished everyone with his world record breaking high jump technique. The Swedes demonstrated a new style in gymnastics.

The athletics were more successful than other events, although they began on the traditional holiday of July 14, when all Paris was celebrating, not competing.

1904 St. Louis: Side show to the World Fair

The third Olympiad was off to a bad start long before the games opened in St. Louis, Missouri, in 1904. The International Olympic Committee had in fact decided in favour of Chicago. But after considerable wrangling, and the arbitration of the US President, Theodore Roosevelt, St. Louis emerged as the next Olympic city.

In spite of the Paris experience, the games were once again to be part of a World Fair. Perhaps because of this unpromising beginning, Coubertin did not cross the Atlantic to watch the games.

All American contests

Practically all the competitors were Americans. Only 496 sportsmen took part. Of these only thirty-two were foreigners and most of them came from Canada. The British were represented by one Irishman!

There was a full range of athletic events and some Americans achieved excellent results. But the promoters of the World Fair insisted on all sorts of side show attractions to thrill the crowds.

Anthropological antics

There were "Anthropological Days", with events like weight lifting for pygmies, boxing for women and many others performed by untrained Red Indians, Negroes, Patagonians and Chinese.

When Coubertin heard about this from members of the IOC reporting after the games, he was not nearly as upset as they were. He foresaw that one day other races of people would give white men serious competition.

With 22 out of 25 possible titles, the Americans did not lack heroes, or competition, even if only amongst themselves. The Irish-American Kiely won the 1904 equivalent of the decathlon, with consistently good results in a vast variety of events: throwing a 56lb stone, the pole vault, the mile, the high jump and the hurdles. No wonder it was called the all-rounder championship!

America's Kiely won the all-rounder championship, which included events like throwing the 56lb stone, the mile and the high jump.

From a standing start

Ray Ewry performed wonders in the standing jumps. Until 1912 the long jump, high jump and triple jump with a run up were separate events. In 1904 Ewry won all three standing jump gold medals: 4ft 11ins in the high jump, 11ft 4½ins in the long jump and 34ft 7½ins in the triple jump.

Missouri businessmen insisted on all sorts of side show attractions in the 1904 games, which were part of the St. Louis World Fair.

Ray Ewry was unbeatable in the standing long jump, high jump and triple jump. Jumps with a run up were separate events.

1904 St. Louis: Marathon winner takes a lift!

The sensation of the St. Louis games was not in the end provided by the promoters of the World Fair. It was the work of the marathon runner Fred Lorz, and there are two sides to his story.

Joke or fraud?

Either Lorz deliberately fell behind, then climbed into a passing car, had himself set down ten kilometres from the finish, so that he could jog casually into the stadium, run a lap of honour and collect the medal. Or he dropped out, took a lift, but the car broke down, and he then decided to continue on for a joke.

Whatever the truth of the matter, he did arrive first, went through the medal ceremony and was being photographed with Alice Roosevelt, daughter of the President, when the next runner, Thomas Hicks, entered the stadium completely exhausted.

At that point the judges who had followed the race arrived too and confirmed that Lorz had not run all the way. He was disqualified and disgraced.

However, by today's rules, Hicks would have been disqualified too. He only managed to complete the race with the help of injections and brandy, but in 1904 there were no anti-doping regulations.

Lorz was allowed to compete again several years later, and proved that he was no mean marathonist by winning the United States Championship convincingly.

Swimmers take a ducking

There were upsets too in the swimming pool, which was in fact a lake. The start was made from a pontoon which upended and sank when competitors dived off it. There were several events which would not be recognised today, but few startling efforts.

Two swimmers stood out, the American, Daniels, who dominated the 220 and 440 yards and a Hungarian Halmay who won the 50 and 100 yards.

Absent record holder

In the stadium the Americans continued their almost unchallenged run of victories. Archie Hahn set a time of 21.6sec for the 200m, which was amazing for 1904. He also won the 100m with the not so good time of 12sec.

Myer Prinstein took the long jump title with an impressive 24ft 1in, which would probably have been better had his arch-rival, the world record holder, O'Connor of Ireland, been at the games.

American marathonist Lorz took a lift and was disqualified. Winner Hicks (USA) took brandy on the way.

Swimming events were held in a lake. The start was made from a pontoon which sank. Archie Hahn (USA) took the 200m title in the excellent time of 21.6sec. He also won the 100m in 12sec.

932
803

1908 London: Miracles at short notice

With little to show from the disappointments of Paris and St. Louis, the Olympic movement was still frail and far from well-established at the beginning of the 20th century.

After the debacle in America, an IOC meeting in London appointed Rome the next Olympic city. Two years later, another blow fell: the Italians could not stage the games after all. London was to take over at short notice.

London takes over

The British Olympic Committee had been formed in 1905 and under Lord Desborough, they performed miracles.

A new stadium was built at Shepherd's Bush. There were facilities for cycling and swimming as well as athletics and the whole programme contained 21 competitions.

In fact the sheer number of events caused considerable confusion in the arena, and some discontented murmurs were heard in the crowd. Tickets were expensive, but this did not stop a capacity audience of 90,000 turning up on the last day.

Mel Sheppard (USA) was the hero of the games. He won both the 800m and the 1,500m, in which he outstripped Britain's Harold Wilson.

One man race

The Americans had a powerful team, winning 15 gold medals, but they did not have everything their own way. In the 400m three Americans, Carpenter, Robbins and Taylor defeated Halswelle of England. But the judges ruled that Carpenter had obstructed the Englishman, that he should be disqualified and that the race should be re-run without him. The other two Americans stood by their team-mate and refused to comply, leaving Halswelle a solitary run to victory in a one-man race.

The high jump was another controversial event, but this time an American, Porter, took the honours. Three men shared second place, Leahy (GB), Somodi (Hung.), and André (France).

Enter the ladies

It was in 1908 that women were allowed to compete in the Olympics for the first time. Thirty six of them took part, but they were not allowed to receive medals for their efforts — only diplomas.

The un-numbered Olympics

Some of the athletes who appeared in London had also been to the so-called interim games in Athens in 1906. Coubertin agreed that the Greeks could hold the extra games, but they were never officially included in the number of modern Olympiads, although they were more international than the 1904 games had been.

Lord Desborough's British Olympic Committee took over from the Italians with only two years to prepare for the games. A new stadium was built with a pool in the centre.

Halswelle of England ran to gold on his own – his American competitors had been disqualified. Porter (USA) won the high jump. Three men tied for second place.

Mel Sheppard (USA) was the hero of the games, winning both the 800m and the 1,500m.

1908 London: British victories — with help

As in many Olympiads since, local performers put up a spirited show. The Americans, as usual, took home the largest number of medals, but the British gave them strong competition.

The rowing was held at Henley, where Britain profited from the fact that the Americans had been unable to bring their own boats with them across the Atlantic. On their home ground British oarsmen won every event, although in the eights the Belgians came close to victory.

Victories for home team

British boxers did well too, taking the titles in all five weight categories. In the cycling Britons took gold medals in the team event, the 5km, 10km and 20km races.

In the 100m swimming pool, specially built into the centre of the stadium, Taylor and Holman brought Britain more medals, and the home team won the water polo as well. Add to that clean sweeps in sailing and tennis (in which Charlotte Cooper was the first lady to win an Olympic title), wins in football, hockey and shooting, plus three wrestling events, and it is not difficult to imagine that there was a little envious resentment among other athletes.

Unfair judges

The Americans, with some justification, thought that the English judges were not always fair. Certainly some of their decisions were controversial. Others were made difficult by the confusion of so many events taking place simultaneously. For a long time after the games were over, relations between British and American athletics organisations were extremely frosty, with both sides publishing accusations and counter-criticism.

Marathon winner disqualified

The last event on the programme was the marathon and this turned out to be one of the most controversial of all races. Hefferon of South Africa had been expected to lead into the stadium, but the Italian Dorando Pietri staggered in, with Hayes of America second. Pietri fell five times in the last 400 yards and needed medical treatment before he could finish. He fell again only five yards out, and was helped over the line by a judge and a journalist.

Pietri was disqualified, in spite of protesting that he had not asked for help, and Hayes was declared the winner. But public feeling was on Pietri's side. After the Italian had recovered, he was presented with a magnificent cup by Queen Alexandra.

The Italian Pietri was helped over the line in the marathon, and so disqualified.

Public opinion was on Pietri's side and Queen Alexandra gave him a special cup.

Hayes (USA) was given the marathon title. The Americans complained British judges were biased.

1912 Stockholm: The Olympics come of age

Olympianism has been well-served by Scandinavia. The Stockholm games of 1912 rank only with the Helsinki games of 1952 as the most harmonious and least controversial of the modern era.

London had set the Olympics on the right path, but it took the Swedes to make sure that the movement would never look back, even through two world wars. For the first time Coubertin was truly satisfied by the games.

Advantages of Empire

Once again the Americans dominated events, taking 26 gold medals, and once again the local team did well. Sweden collected 23 golds. Britain came third in the medal table with only 10, a fact that led Sir Arthur Conan Doyle to suggest that a British Empire team should be fielded in future!

The men's 100m produced the nearest thing to an incident seen in Stockholm. The American, Drew, was favourite, but in the heats he ruptured an achilles tendon. When he did not appear for the final there were malicious rumours that he had been locked in the dressing room to prevent a black man winning. When the final did take place, there were seven false starts. The eventual winner was Craigh (USA) with a time of 10.8sec.

Bright Path to misfortune

Jim Thorpe was the outstanding athlete of the games. He was an American Indian, whose tribal name was Bright Path. He won both the pentathlon and the decathlon by huge margins. Gustav, King of Sweden, congratulated him on his victories with the accolade: 'Sir, you are the best athlete in the world.'

However, the future was not to be so bright for Thorpe. Soon after the games he was disqualified and deprived of his medals because at one time he had played with a small professional baseball team, to help pay for his studies. It was only on his deathbed, 41 years later, that his amateur status was restored to him. Discussions still continue about re-awarding him his medals.

British track golds

Although the Americans and Finns (unwillingly still competing as part of the Russian Empire) took most of the track titles, the British were not completely outclassed. In the 1,500m Jackson overtook three Americans in the final ten yards, becoming the first Olympic runner to beat the four minute barrier at that distance.

The British team of D'Arcy, Applegarth, McIntosh and Jacobs were the last non-Americans to win the 4 x 100m relay until 1960.

Drew (USA) was 100m favourite but was injured. Rumours circulated that he had been locked in the dressing room to stop a black man winning. In the final there were seven false starts.

Jim Thorpe won the decathlon, but was disqualified. On his deathbed his amateur status was restored to him, but not his medals.

1912 Stockholm: Sportsmanship, but no quarter

The most dramatic race of the Stockholm Olympics involved a Finn, Hannes Kolehmainen, and a Frenchman, Jean Bouin. In the final these two soon left the rest of the field, headed by Hutson of Britain, far behind.

The crowd joins in

To riotous acclaim from the crowd Kolehmainen and Bouin ran side by side down the final straight. Only 10 metres from the tape the Finn passed the Frenchman on the outside. The world record had been broken by almost half a minute and now stood at 14mins 36.6sec. Bouin and Hutson were killed, only days apart, on the Western Front in October 1914.

No race without the Duke

The first of the long line of American swimming champions appeared at Stockholm, Duke Kohanamoku, from Honolulu. His magnificent style was something new to swimming and his only rival was Cecil Healey of Australia.

Unfortunately there was a misunderstanding about the starting time of the 100m, and Kohanamoku arrived too late. Healey sportingly announced that, if 'the Duke' was not going to swim, nor would he. Race officials relented, and Kohanamoku won the 100m in 1min 3.4sec.

Water sports apparently suited British sportsmen and women of the period. The men claimed the water polo and the women the first Olympic women's 4 x 100m freestyle relay. Still in the water, Kinnear (GB) won the sculls and Britain took first and second places in the eights.

Wrestling until they drop

In the Greco-Roman wrestling there was a contest with political overtones which no doubt made it doubly hard-fought. The Russian, Klein, and the Finn, Asikainen, met in the middleweight semi-final and battled it out for 11 hours. Eventually the Finn fell and his Russian conqueror dropped beside him.

Klein was so exhausted that he was obliged to forfeit his match against the Swede, Johansson, who thus won the gold medal without a fight.

When the games came to a triumphant end, Coubertin looked forward to peaceful times and the next Games in Berlin. But his hopes were not realised. There was no sixth Olympiad of the modern era.

The most dramatic race in Stockholm involved a duel between Bouin (France) and Kolehmainen (Finland), who won the 5,000m.

Gallant Australian Healey refused to compete without his arch-rival Kohanamoku (USA), who had been disqualified. The American won the 100m freestyle.

Records and results: 1896 – 1912

Old time events

Competitions staged in the early Olympics, but no longer on the programme.

1896

Men's rope climbing (also held in 1904, 1924 and 1932).
Tennis (also from 1904-1924).
Cycling, 12 hour race: A. Schmal of Austria covered 315km (196.8 miles).

1900

Swimming, 4km freestyle.
Athletics: 60m men's sprint, standing high jump, standing long jump, standing triple jump, tug of war.
Cricket and croquet were played.
Live pigeon shooting, underwater swimming, long jump and high jump for horses were also on the programme.

1904

Putting the weight (56lbs, 25.5kg) winner, E. Desmarteau (Canada), 34ft 4ins (10.46m).
Club swinging: winner E. Hennig (USA).
There was also a golf championship.

1908

Polo (held in each succeeding games until 1936).
Rugby Union 1908 winners: Australia; 1920 and 1924: USA
Gold medals were awarded for lacrosse and motor boat racing.

1912

Cross country, individual and team.
Throwing the discus, left and right handed: winner, A.R. Taipale (Finland), 271ft 8¼ins (82.86m), combined distance.
Throwing the javelin, left and right handed: winner, J.J. Saaristo (Finland), 358ft 11ins (109.42m), combined distance.
Shot put left and right handed: winner, Ralph Rose (USA) 90ft 10ins (27.7m), combined distance.
From 1912 to 1948 gold medals were awarded for architecture, literature, sculpture, painting and music. In 1912 Coubertin won a literature prize under an assumed name.
In 1948 A.R. Thompson (GB), who was deaf and dumb, won the painting medal.

The three Irish whales

Three Irish-Americans, born within a few miles of each other in the counties of Limerick and Tipperary, all became world beating hammer throwers.

1900

winner, John J. Flanagan (USA), 163ft 1½ins (49.73m), new Olympic record.

1904

winner, John J. Flanagan (USA), 168ft 0½ins (51.23m) new Olympic record.

1908

winner, John J. Flanagan (USA), 170ft 4ins (51.92m), new Olympic record.
second, Matt McGrath (USA), 167ft 11ins (51.18m).

1912

winner, Matt McGrath (USA), 179ft 7ins (54.74m), new Olympic record.

1920

winner, Pat Ryan (USA), 173ft 5½ins (52.87m).

1908: Fair play by the judges?

British judges were supposed to be impartial. Yet Britain won half the events, causing great controversy.

Sport	Total gold	GB gold
Archery	3	3
Athletics	28	8
Boxing	5	5
Cycling	7	5
Fencing	4	–
Football	1	1
Gymnastics	2	-
Hockey	1	1
Lawn and real tennis	7	6
Polo	1	1
Rackets	2	2
Rowing	4	4
Shooting	10	3
Swimming	10	5
Wrestling	9	3
Yachting, motorboating	3	2
Totals	**97**	**49**

King of the standing jumps

Ray Ewry (USA) was paralysed as a boy, but in his Olympic career, 1900-1908, he took ten gold medals, including two he won at the 'un-numbered' 1906 games in Athens.

1900

Standing high jump, 5ft 5ins (1.65m)
Standing long jump, 10ft 6ins (3.2m)
Standing triple jump, distance not recorded.

1904

Standing high jump, 4ft 11ins (1.5m)
Standing long jump, 11ft 4⅞ins (3.47m)
Standing triple jump, distance not recorded.

1906

Standing high jump, distance not recorded.
Standing long jump, distance not recorded.

1908

Standing high jump, 5ft 2ins (1.57m)
Standing long jump, 10ft 11¼ins (3.35m)

1912: The greatest athlete in the world

Jim Thorpe, an American Indian, was thought by King Gustav of Sweden to be the greatest athlete in the world. He won both the decathlon and the pentathlon in Stockholm. His decathlon record stood for 15 years. These are his results:

100m, 10.9sec
400m, 48.7sec
1,500m, 4mins 40.1sec
110m hurdles, 15sec (equalled world record)
shot put, 47ft 9ins (14.55m)
discus, 125ft 8ins (38.30m)
javelin, 163ft (49.69m)
long jump, 23ft 6ins (7.17m)
high jump, 6ft 5ins (1.96m)
pole vault, 10ft 6ins (3.26m)

How accurate were they?

To start with Olympic results were recorded without any great attention to detail. The stopwatch age did not begin until 1932, and as late as 1956 a photo finish showed that Baker (USA) was second in the 100m to Morrow (USA) by two metres, but both men were given the same time.

1896

In the 800m Demitrios Golemis (Greece) won the bronze medal, coming '90m behind' the winner Ed Flask (USA).

1900

Francis Jarvis (USA) won the 100m in 11sec. As the timing was only accurate to one fifth of a second, Walter Tewksbury (USA) was given second place '1 foot behind', beating Stan Rowley (Australia) 'by inches'.

Top left: British high jumper at 1908 games. No landing mats were used.

Top right: The 1912 British tug-of-war team.

Centre left: Ladies' gymnastics in 1908 at Shepherd's Bush, London.

Bottom left: Dorando Pietri, the ill-fated marathon runner of 1908, being helped over the line, as a result of which he was disqualified.

Centre right: Albert Hill, Britain's king of the middle distances, who won two gold medals in 1920,

Above: Richard Meade (GB) competing in the 3-day event in Montreal.

Left: Rodney Pattisson and Chris Davies (GB) winning the Flying Dutchman class at Kiel in 1972.

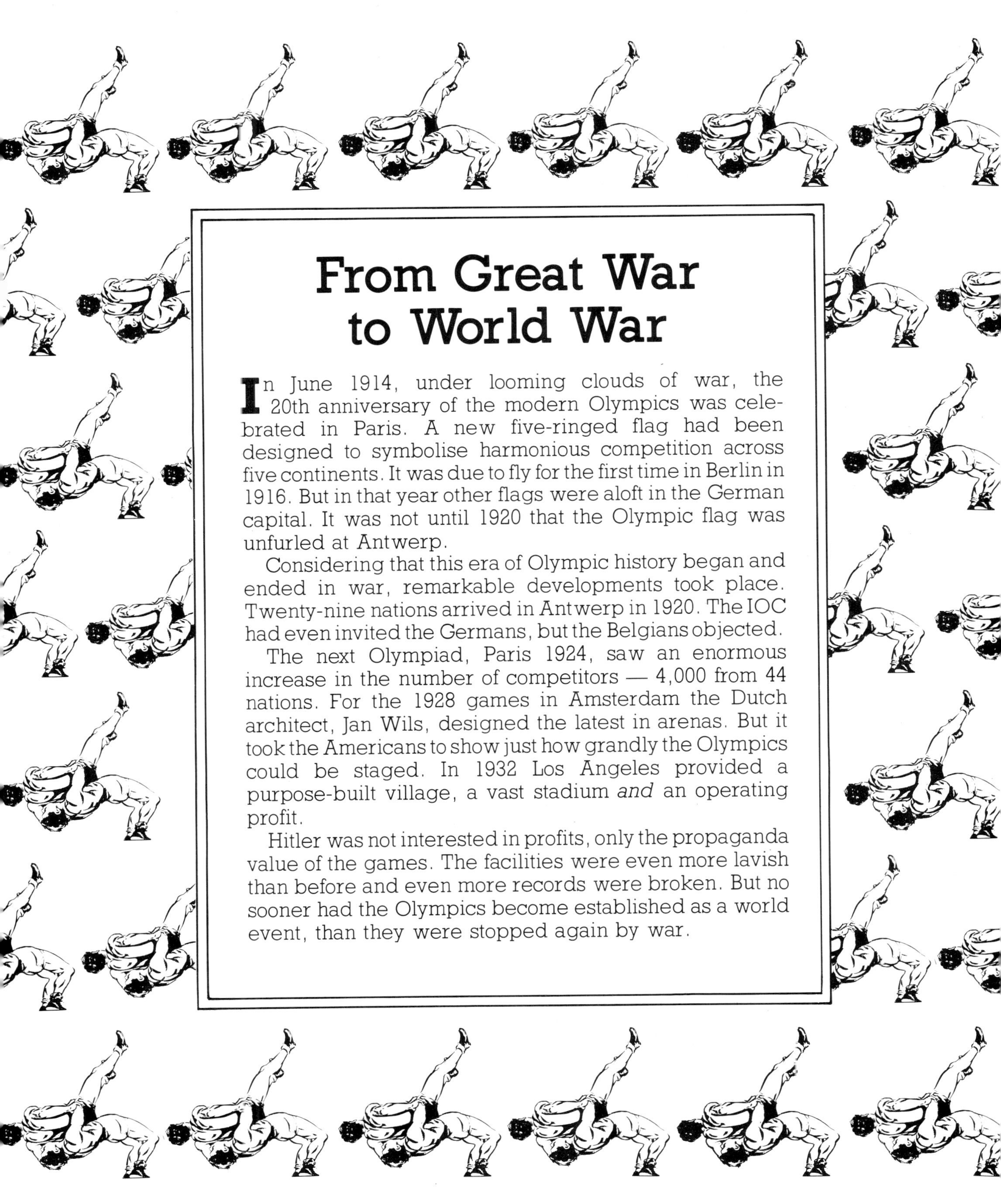

From Great War to World War

In June 1914, under looming clouds of war, the 20th anniversary of the modern Olympics was celebrated in Paris. A new five-ringed flag had been designed to symbolise harmonious competition across five continents. It was due to fly for the first time in Berlin in 1916. But in that year other flags were aloft in the German capital. It was not until 1920 that the Olympic flag was unfurled at Antwerp.

Considering that this era of Olympic history began and ended in war, remarkable developments took place. Twenty-nine nations arrived in Antwerp in 1920. The IOC had even invited the Germans, but the Belgians objected.

The next Olympiad, Paris 1924, saw an enormous increase in the number of competitors — 4,000 from 44 nations. For the 1928 games in Amsterdam the Dutch architect, Jan Wils, designed the latest in arenas. But it took the Americans to show just how grandly the Olympics could be staged. In 1932 Los Angeles provided a purpose-built village, a vast stadium *and* an operating profit.

Hitler was not interested in profits, only the propaganda value of the games. The facilities were even more lavish than before and even more records were broken. But no sooner had the Olympics become established as a world event, than they were stopped again by war.

1920 Antwerp: The legacy of the First World War

When the International Olympic Committee met in 1914, a new flag had been presented to them. It carried five circles to signify the Olympic brotherhood spanning five continents. It was to have flown for the first time at the 1916 games in Berlin. But the Great War upset the IOC's plans.

The 1920 games had been scheduled for Budapest, but none of the defeated nations was allowed to compete and the games were switched to Antwerp, Belgium. And even there the shadow of war persisted. The US team travelled to the games in a troopship, and when they arrived they found that their accommodation, in a school, was just as uncomfortable. The entire team threatened to boycott the Olympics. So much for international brotherhood!

The Finnish decade opens

Athletes from 29 countries took part in the opening ceremony. The oath of amateurism was taken for the first time. A man named Paavo Nurmi brought a new dimension to running — it was the start of a decade of Finnish athletic superiority. In the 5,000m he finished second to the Frenchman, Joseph Guillemot, but then the 23-year old Finn reeled off the 10,000m, the cross country, and led Finland to the cross country team title. Three golds and a silver! At the end of the games Finland and the USA were equal first in the medal table: nine golds each.

Hill's double gold for Britain

Success too for Britain, when Albert Hill achieved the rare double of the 800m and 1,500m gold medals. And Percy Hodges (GB) won the steeplechase in 10min 0.4sec — not bad for 1920.

Kelly — the artisan oarsman

In 1912 an Irish-American oarsman named Kelly had been refused permission to row at Henley, because he worked with his hands. John Kelly took sweet revenge by winning the single and double sculls at Antwerp. In the singles he beat the prince of British scullers, Jack Beresford. Kelly's son went on to row in the Royal Regatta at Henley and his daughter, Grace, became a Princess in her own right.

In 1914, the IOC approved the new flag, symbolising Olympic brotherhood over five continents. Because of the war it was not used until 1920 in Antwerp, where Albert I, King of Belgium opened the games.

Paavo Nurmi, the greatest of the Flying Finns, came second in the 5,000m but won three gold medals.

John Kelly had been refused entry to the Henley Regatta in 1912. In 1920 he won two sculling gold medals.

1920 Antwerp: A golden gesture

One of the strangest victories in the history of the Olympics occurred in the 1,500m, when Albert Hill completed the middle-distance double. He had luck on his side in the 800m and won after the favourite, Bevil Rudd of South Africa, stumbled into a pothole when clear in the lead. Rudd staggered on over the final 80m to take the bronze.

Noel Baker's sacrifice

Victory in that race made Hill clear favourite for the 'metric mile', but on the final lap it was another English runner, Philip Noel Baker, who appeared to have the race in his grasp. The sparse crowd stared in disbelief when Noel Baker allowed his countryman a clear run to the tape for victory in 4mins 1 8sec. Noel Baker, who later won a Nobel Prize and became a member of the 1945 Labour Government, was obviously pleased his rival had done the double in British colours.

Hill was 36 at the time. He had served the full four years of the war and had the knack of being able to sleep for two or three hours before a big race. He was always the most relaxed man in the field.

The fastest man on earth

As ever, the sprints captured the crowd's imagination. Charley Paddock (USA) lived up to his reputation of being the fastest man on earth. He won the 100m in 10.8sec raising his arms in victory four strides from the tape. He did the same in the 200m — but this time it was a premature gesture. Striding up to him at that moment was his American team-mate, Allen Woodring, the eventual winner.

After the 200m, the organisers, worried by the pathetically small crowds, opened the gates to anyone who wished to watch. But only the football final attracted a capacity 45,000 crowd. Belgium beat Spain 3-0. And who won the rugby title? The USA by beating France by 8pts to nil!

One man had to win his event twice to get the gold medal. At the pool the Hawaian American, Duke Paoa Kahanamoko, won the 100m freestyle only to hear the race declared void. He promptly repeated his effort in a world record 1min 0.4sec to take the gold. He later became sheriff of Honolulu.

Albert Hill of Britain scored a double victory in the 800m and the 1,500m. Philip Noel Baker, later to be a government minister and Nobel Prize winner, was leading in the 1,500m, but allowed Hill through to take his second gold medal.

Charley Paddock (USA) took a victory leap over the line in the 100m.

1924 Paris: Coubertin's last games

With the memories of the war receding, Austria, Hungary, Bulgaria and Turkey took their places at the opening ceremony at the Colombes Stadium. Germany was still absent, because of the tension surrounding the payment of war reparations to France.

Forty four nations took part and the games were held in Paris at the express request of the Baron de Coubertin, to mark the 30th anniversary of the foundation of the modern Olympics. For the first time the athletes were all housed together — and still the Americans were dissatisfied. Accommodation consisted of wooden huts — a far cry from today's luxurious Olympic villages.

Nurmi at his greatest

The young and inexperienced Paavo Nurmi of the Antwerp games had now become the athlete who dominated spectators' conversations and his rivals' thoughts. In the space of 1hr 45mins the Flying Finn took the 1,500m and the 5,000m, setting Olympic records at each distance. Then, in temperatures of over 90 deg F (32 deg C), he slaughtered the opposition in the cross country and again led the Finns to team victory. In the 3,000m team event he collected his fifth gold medal of the games.

No Sunday running

The Scot Eric Liddell had won the bronze medal in the 200m, and he was expected to do better in the 100m. But as the final was on Sunday he withdrew on religious grounds. However, Britain still took the title. Londoner, Harold Abrahams, won the gold with a time of 10.6sec.
He is still the only Briton to have won at that distance. And Liddell still got his gold. In the 400m he beat the American, Horatio Fitch, in a world record time of 47.6sec. Guy Butler (GB) was third.

Coubertin says goodbye

The man who finished third in the pentathlon, Bob Gendre (USA) broke the long jump world record (7m 76.5) — 32cms further than the winner of the long jump title!

At the closing ceremony Coubertin said farewell. These were the last games he attended.

Eric Liddell, although favourite, refused to compete in the 100m on a Sunday. He won the 400m, while Harold Abrahams (GB) won the 100m.

In Paris Paavo Nurmi of Finland reached the peak of his Olympic career. He collected five gold medals, with two Olympic records in two hours.

Coubertin particularly wanted the 1924 games to be held in Paris. This was the last Olympiad he witnessed.

1928 Amsterdam: New heroes for old

The games of the ninth Olympiad in Amsterdam saw the glory of Nurmi fade. He won the 10,000m and took a silver behind another Finn, Ville Ritola, in the 5,000m.

But as Nurmi departed, so another Olympic hero was born — Johnny Weissmuller. This good-looking all-American athlete had won three swimming golds in Paris in 1924. This time he won the 100m and led the USA home in the sprint relay. Then he packed his bags for Hollywood to become the first and most famous Tarzan of the Apes. It wasn't until 1964 that another swimmer managed to win three Olympic 100m in a row — Australian Dawn Fraser.

Training in the mud

Douglas Lowe, whose early experience of athletics consisted of running on the muddy football pitch of north London's Highgate School, had surprised many people by winning the 800m in Paris. Now as a much more experienced runner, he successfully defended his title. Only two other athletes have equalled this Olympic feat. Another British victory came in the 400m hurdles through Lord Burghley, later to become a member of the IOC.

Enter the ladies

The Dutch had built a magnificent stadium. The Germans were back, but still controversy surrounded the games. Coubertin stayed away, largely because he frowned on women competitors becoming fully involved in the Olympics. In Amsterdam they were to compete in the athletics for the first time. The Americans were still causing problems over the facilities — this time they actually rammed the gates of the stadium with a car in order to get inside and train.

The Dutch authorities had closed their splendid new stadium until the official opening. The athletes wished to train in it, so some Americans rammed the gates in a car.

Lowe (GB) defended the 800m title he had won in Paris.

Oda scored Japan's first field gold. Weissmuller left swimming to act the part of Tarzan.

Finns to the fore

Japan made her first mark on the games when Mikio Oda took the triple jump gold medal. Paddy O'Callaghan of Ireland hurled the hammer into top position. On the track the Finnish runners won the 1,500m, the 5,000m and the 10,000m and took the first three places in the steeplechase. Uraguay won the football for the second successive games and two years later won the inaugural World Cup.

The Finns took the first three places in the steeplechase.

1932 Los Angeles: Depression and extravaganza

Apart from the all-American fiasco at Saint Louis in 1904, this was the first time the games had been held outside Europe. Los Angeles was the host city. The depression was eating away the souls of men and 'Buddy can you spare a dime?' was the song on everyone's lips. Yet in lavish surroundings and glorious weather, world records fell like autumn leaves, and at the end of it all, the organising committee found themselves with a million dollar profit. 1932 began the fashion for the Olympic spectaculars of more recent games.

A stadium for 1984

Athletes found themselves for the first time in a purpose-built village. The stadium was magnificent and so far ahead of its time that with a touch of modernisation it will be used again for the 1984 games. There was grandeur and opulence everywhere, in marked contrast to the harrowed faces of Americans outside sunny California.

The end of an era

Things weren't much better in Ireland, but Paddy O'Callaghan repeated his hammer victory and the Finns were once again out in force: one, two and three in the javelin; Volmari Iso-Hollo first in the steeplechase; two medals in the 5,000m and 10,000m; silvers in the hammer and decathlon and bronze in the marathon.

But one famous blue and white vest was missing. Paavo Nurmi, still perhaps the greatest Olympian of them all, was banned for professionalism. The International Amateur Athletic Federation claimed he had pocketed over-generous expenses while competing in Germany. The Finnish Association disagreed, but the IOC supported the IAAF and Nurmi, now 35, did not run. Nurmi was sickened by what he saw as an injustice, became a hermit from the sport — rarely even watching athletics — and ran his tie shop in Helsinki. Most observers believed Nurmi's side of the story.

The magnificent stadium built for 1932 will serve again in 1984.

In spite of the depression Los Angeles put on the most lavish Olympics to date. One great name was absent. Nurmi had been banned for professionalism – a charge he always disputed.

1932 Los Angeles: The greatest foot race ever run

When the competitions started, Nurmi and the depression were forgotten by the fans who packed the venues. For the fourth successive games an Englishman stood on the winner's rostrum after the 800m. This time it was Tommy Hampson and he had to break the world record to strike gold.

Three outstanding Americans, two Canadians, two Britons and Otto Pelzer of Germany reached the final. Phil Edwards of Canada reached the bell in the then unbelievable time of 52.7sec in a bid to burn off his rivals. With 100m left Edwards was still out in front, but then Hampson, who had been 20m down at the halfway mark, unleashed his telling sprint. He won in 1min 49.8sec and promptly collapsed with fatigue. The athlete Lord Burghley said that he had never seen a race like it. Neither had Hampson — he beat his previous best by 2.4 sec!

First photo finish

The camera came into use for the first time to decide a winner, and of course it had to be in the 100m. The naked eye and stopwatch could not separate the Americans Eddie Toland and Ralph Metcalfe. But newsreel film was offered to the judges and after several hours Tolan got the gold although both broke the world record at 10.3sec. Tolan went on to prove his mastery in the 200m in 21.2sec.

In the 400m hurdles the Irishman Bob Tisdall won the gold, but the second man home, Glenn Hardin (USA) broke the world record with 52sec. Tisdall's 51.8sec was disqualified because he put down a hurdle.

Japanese invade the pool

Nations preparing for war, or ruled on military lines, have a habit of excelling at the Olympics. And Japan's militaristic attitude was reflected in the swimming events. Yasuji Miyazaki (16) won the 100m freestyle and Kusuo Kitamura (14) took the 1,500m. The Japanese won five of the six swimming gold medals, plus four silvers and two bronzes. Soon the armies of Japan would be marching through Manchuria and across China.

Britain's Tommy Hampson collapsed after winning the 800m.

Bob Tisdall (Eire) won the 400m hurdles. Hardin (USA) came second and took the world record.

The Japanese showed a preview of their military might with impressive swimming results – five out of six golds.

1932 Los Angeles: The women's events come of age

The partial eclipse of the Rising Sun occurred in the 400m when Buster Crabbe (USA) used his enormous muscle power and endless training to effect and won in 4mins 48.4sec. He was to follow Johnny Weissmuller in the part of Tarzan on the Hollywood screen.

Babe, the world-beater

Women's athletics, still the Cinderella of the games, attracted big and enthusiastic crowds. And the development in the four previous years was illustrated by new world records in every single event.

The heroine of the games was Mildred Didriksen (USA). She complained bitterly at being allowed to enter only three events. But Babe set world records in them all! She won the 80m hurdles in 11.7sec, the javelin with a throw of 43m 68cm, and cleared the same height as the winner, Jean Shiley (USA), in the high jump . . . 1m 65cm. Babe also cleared 2cm higher but was disqualified because her head crossed the bar first.

Later as Babe Zaharias she became the best woman golfer of her day and then told the world her next competition was against cancer which she fought courageously to the end.

Which colours to run in?

The problem of athletes born in one country and brought up in another was highlighted at Los Angeles. The Americans assumed Cleveland's Stella Walsh would win the 100m for them. They were partly right — as Stanislawa Walasiewicz she clocked a world record 11.9sec, but wearing the colours of Poland!

No problems, though, for the Swedish wrestler, Carl Westergren. He was one of the most experienced Olympians in Los Angeles. He had won the middleweight title in 1920, the light heavyweight gold in 1924 and now he crowned his 12-year career with the heavyweight title — growing with each games!

The first modern games

There had been many mistakes made at the games — the steeplechasers ran one lap too many; wrong placings were announced for contestants; the recall gun often misfired after false starts. But these games marked the beginning of the Olympics as we know them, for good or ill. Gone were the days of merely taking part. Winning at all costs had become the name of the games.

Swedish wrestler Carl Westergren had competed in three games at three different weights and won gold in each of them.

Babe Didriksen (USA) was the best of a good turn out of women athletes. She set three new world records in the 80m hurdles, javelin and high jump.

Buster Crabbe (USA) was the only male swimmer to stand out against the Japanese. He won the 400m gold.

306
92
JAMAICA
574

1936 Berlin: The Hitler games

Beneath the shadow of the swastika the youth of the world assembled for the games of the eleventh Olympiad. The Olympic lamb entered the lair of the Nazi wolf, Berlin, where the most chauvinistic and politically motivated games on record took place. While Adolph Hitler greeted the world in the Reich Stadion, his henchmen were beating people to death. The aryans were destined to dominate the world; Jews and negroes were second class people. So ran the Nazi theory.

The German military machine was evident everywhere, backed by men in SS uniforms and the brown-shirted SA. The cry was 'Seig Heil'. The Germans were demonstrating their superiority to the rest of the world.

The first flame

An impressive new ceremony was added to the programme. A torch, lit on Mount Olympus, was carried by a series of runners to Berlin. The wonderful stadium held 110,000 spectators; the athletes' villages surpassed even the grandeur of Los Angeles; and for the first time the games were broadcast and televised. Hitler's mistress, Leni Riefenstahl, produced and directed a film of the games. To this day it is still considered one of the finest sports films ever made.

Military bands played in every corner of the capital. Shop windows were full of everything, though inside there was very little. Entertainment of foreign visitors was lavish and Hitler fooled millions into believing that a German economic miracle had taken place in the three years of Nazi rule.

The silent Fuhrer

At the opening ceremony the Fuhrer's speech drifted from Olympic ideals to propaganda. The IOC President, Monsieur Baillet-Latour, forced Hitler to cut short his address. This was probably the last time anyone told Hitler to shut up!

The Germans denied anti-semitism in their team selection. They brought home from America a token Jew, Helene Mayer, who won a silver medal in the fencing.

Hitler used the 1936 games to publicise the supposed achievements of his regime. The IOC President cut short the Fuhrer's propagandist opening speech.

Leni Riefenstahl's epic 4-hour film, Olympische Speile 1936, showed Jesse Owens as hero of the games.

1936 Berlin: Black triumph in the Aryan Olympics

In one of life's sweet ironies the Aryan games were dominated by a black man — James Cleveland Owens. As a boy he introduced himself to his first schoolmistress as 'J.C. Owens'. From then on he was just called Jesse. As a man he set an Olympic record so far unequalled and forced Hitler to show his true face to the world.

The champion snubbed

The Nazi leader was at the Olympic stadium for the long jump competition, where Lutz Long was the big German hope. He actually led the competition for a few minutes, but with his next jump Owens strained every sinew to crash through the 8m barrier for the first time in Olympic history. The gold medal was his.

Hitler's face dropped and the packed stadium fell silent. Hitler looked at the sky and decided it would rain. He left the stadium and snubbed the greatest champion of all.

Unequalled record

Jesse Owens, that same day, went on to win the 200m in 20.7sec. He had already won the 100m in 10.3sec — having set a world record of 10.2sec in the heats — and was also a member of the US sprint relay team which struck gold. Four gold medals therefore went home in Owen's bag and no other sprinter has ever matched that.

On the day of his long jump success he had also to compete in heats for the 200m. In the final he seemed lethargic for the first 100 metres. Matthew Robinson towed the finalists into the home stretch, but then Jess lengthened his stride in almost lazy fashion and zipped away from his rivals.

Long's sportsmanship

Hitler and Nazism apart, Owens remembers the sporting way Long contested the long jump. 'He treated me as a man, as a rival and was first to shake me by the hand afterwards. We became good friends,' Owens recalls.

Owens soon turned professional and since the war he has been a regular member of the Olympic press corps. He has lost nothing of his youthful charm. Here is a king who has always worn his crown with dignity.

Hitler believed the Germans, the Aryan race would dominate the games. Jesse Owens proved him wrong.

Owens won four golds: 100m, 200m relay and long jump, beating Lutz of Germany.

1936 Berlin: An All Black beats the world's best

From the gently rolling Canterbury Plain, buttressed to the west by the Southern Alps and kissed by the blue Pacific on the east, came an All Black. Born of English stock in New Zealand, tempered in Timaru, refined at Oxford University and triumphant in Berlin. We may never see his like again — Jack Lovelock.

In the years leading up to Berlin, Lovelock had raced against the best milers in the world — Wooderson and Cornes from England, Cunningham and Bonthron (USA), Ny of Sweden, Beccali of Italy and Goix of France. He had won and lost against them individually until Berlin. Then he beat the lot.

The master tactician

Some say only the Chataway-Kuts race in London in 1954 rivalled the race seen in Berlin over 1,500m. Wooderson was injured and did not make the final, but Cornes took the early running with Cunningham and Beccali close behind. Then Cunningham went with Lovelock, the master tactician, in second spot. Beccali third. Ny came to join Cunningham and at the bell the Swede took over.

Lovelock was about to pounce when he noticed Cunningham waiting for the move, so the New Zealander waited. Cat and mouse round the bend into the back-straight. Then off; Lovelock on his own with 300m to go; victory in a world record 3mins 47.8sec. The first NZ athlete to win an Olympic gold medal.

Tragically, Lovelock suffered a series of dizzy spells in New York in December 1949 and during one of them he fell beneath a subway train at Church Avenue station, Brooklyn.

A British tradition

The tradition of British quarter-miling continued in Berlin with Godfrey Brown defying all the odds and splitting the American runners Archie Williams and Jim Lu Valle. Brown was just two tenths of a second away from gold. But even more unexpectedly he anchored the 400m relay to claim a gold medal after Wolff, Rampling and Roberts had maintained contact with the Americans on the previous legs.

Dropped from the team

One American who lost contact with her team was swimmer Eleanor Jarrett, who had rows with officials during the voyage to Europe and was dropped from the team. She was expected to win the 100m backstroke title, which subsequently went to Dina Senff of the Netherlands.

The marathon was run through the cobbled streets of Berlin. Kitei Son came from Korea, but ran in Japanese colours, as his country was occupied by the Japanese. With his team-mate Shoryu Nan, he set a crisp pace. A lone Englishman, Ernest Harper took up the challenge, but by the halfway mark, Son was in command. However, Nan could not catch Harper for second spot.

Jack Lovelock was the first New Zealander to win an Olympic gold medal, with a memorable 1,500m. His masterful tactics gave him victory over the world's best milers.

Harper (GB) came second to Kitei Son (Japan) in a memorable marathon.

Eleanor Jarrett, the US swimmer, was dropped from the team because of a disagreement with team managers

Records and results: 1920-1936

1924 and 1928, the first Tarzan

Johnny Weissmuller, who later played the part of Tarzan of the Apes in Hollywood films, dominated Olympic swimming events for two games. Here are his results:

1924 Paris

100m freestyle
1. Johnny Weissmuller (USA) 59 sec, new Olympic record.
2. Duke Kahanamoku (USA) 1min 01.4sec.
3. Sam Kahanamoku (USA) 1min 01.8sec.

400m freestyle
1. Johnny Weissmuller (USA) 5mins 04.2sec.
2. Arne Borg (Sweden) 5mins 05.6sec.
3. Andrew Charlton (Australia) 5mins 06.6sec.

4 x 400m freestyle relay
1. USA (O'Connor, Glancy, Breyer, Weissmuller) 9mins 53.4sec, new Olympic record.
2. Australia 10mins 02.2sec.
3. Sweden 10mins 06.8sec.

1928 Amsterdam

100m freestyle
1. Johnny Weissmuller (USA) 58.6sec, new Olympic record.
2. Istvan Barany (Hungary) 59.8sec.
3. Katsuo Takaishi (Japan) 1min.

4 x 200 freestyle relay
1. USA (Clapp, Laufer, Kojac, Weissmuller) 9mins 32.6sec, new Olympic record.
2. Japan 9mins 44.1sec.
3. Canada 9mins 47.8sec.

Paavo Nurmi, the first Flying Finn

In 11 years Nurmi broke 19 world records in 13 events: 1,500m, 2,000m, 3,000m, 5,000m, 10,000m, 20km, 4 x 1,500m relay, the one hour race, 1 mile, 2 miles, 3 miles, 6 miles, 10 miles. One of his Finnish national records stood until 1949.

Nurmi's Olympic results

1920

winner, 10,000m (31mins 45.8sec)
winner, individual cross-country
winner, team cross-country
second, 5,000m (15mins)

1924

winner, 1,500m (3mins 53.6sec)
winner, 5,000m (14mins 31.2sec)
winner, 3,000m team race
winner, individual cross-country
winner, team cross-country

1928

winner, 10,000m (30mins 18.8sec)
second, 5,000m (14mins 40sec)
second, steeplechase (9mins 31.2sec)

Individual gold medals: 7
Team gold medals: 2
Silver medals: 3

The Immortal Owens

Teenager James Cleveland Owens went to the Berlin games the holder of seven world records: 100yds, 220yds, 100m, 200m, 220yds hurdles, 200m hurdles and long jump. Six of these records he had set in one day. He won four Olympic golds:

100m (10.3sec) equalled Olympic record.

200m (20.7sec), new Olympic record.

Long jump 26ft 5⅛ins, 8.06m), new Olympic record which remained unbeaten for 24 years.

4 x 100m relay (39.8sec), new Olympic record.

Hockey — six for India

India's formidable reputation as a hockey-playing nation is to a large extent built on a record of six successive Olympic wins.

1928	1. India	2. Holland	3. Germany
1932	1. India	2. Japan	3. USA
1936	1. India	2. Germany	3. Holland
1948	1. India	2. Britain	3. Holland
1952	1. India	2. Holland	3. Britain
1956	1. India	2. Pakistan	3. Germany

The Eights, blue riband of rowing

The Americans have won eleven out of seventeen possible gold medals for the eights, the most prestigious of the rowing events. But in recent years their mastery has been challenged.

1900	USA	6mins 09.8sec
1904	USA	7mins 50 sec
1908	GB	7mins 52 sec
1912	GB	6mins 15 sec
1920	USA	6mins 02.6sec
1924	USA	6mins 33.4sec
1928	USA	6mins 03.2sec
1932	USA	6mins 37.6sec
1936	USA	6mins 25.4sec
1948	USA	5mins 56.7sec
1952	USA	6mins 25.9sec
1956	USA	6mins 35.2sec
1960	Germany	5mins 57.18sec
1964	USA	6mins 18.23sec
1968	West Germany	6mins 07 sec
1972	New Zealand	6mins 08.94sec
1976	East Germany	5mins 58.29sec

Dutch girls triumph

Holland is not famous for its swimmers but in 1936 Hendrika Mastenbroek helped Holland to four golds and a silver.

100m freestyle
1. H. Mastenbroek (Holland) 1min 05.9sec, new Olympic record

400m freestyle
1. H. Mastenbroek (Holland) 5mins 26.4sec, new Olympic record

100m backstroke
1. D. Senff (Holland) 1 min 18.9sec.
2. H. Mastenbroek (Holland) 1min 19.2sec.

4 x 100m freestyle relay
1. Holland 4mins 36sec, new Olympic record.

Basketball 1972, USA v USSR.

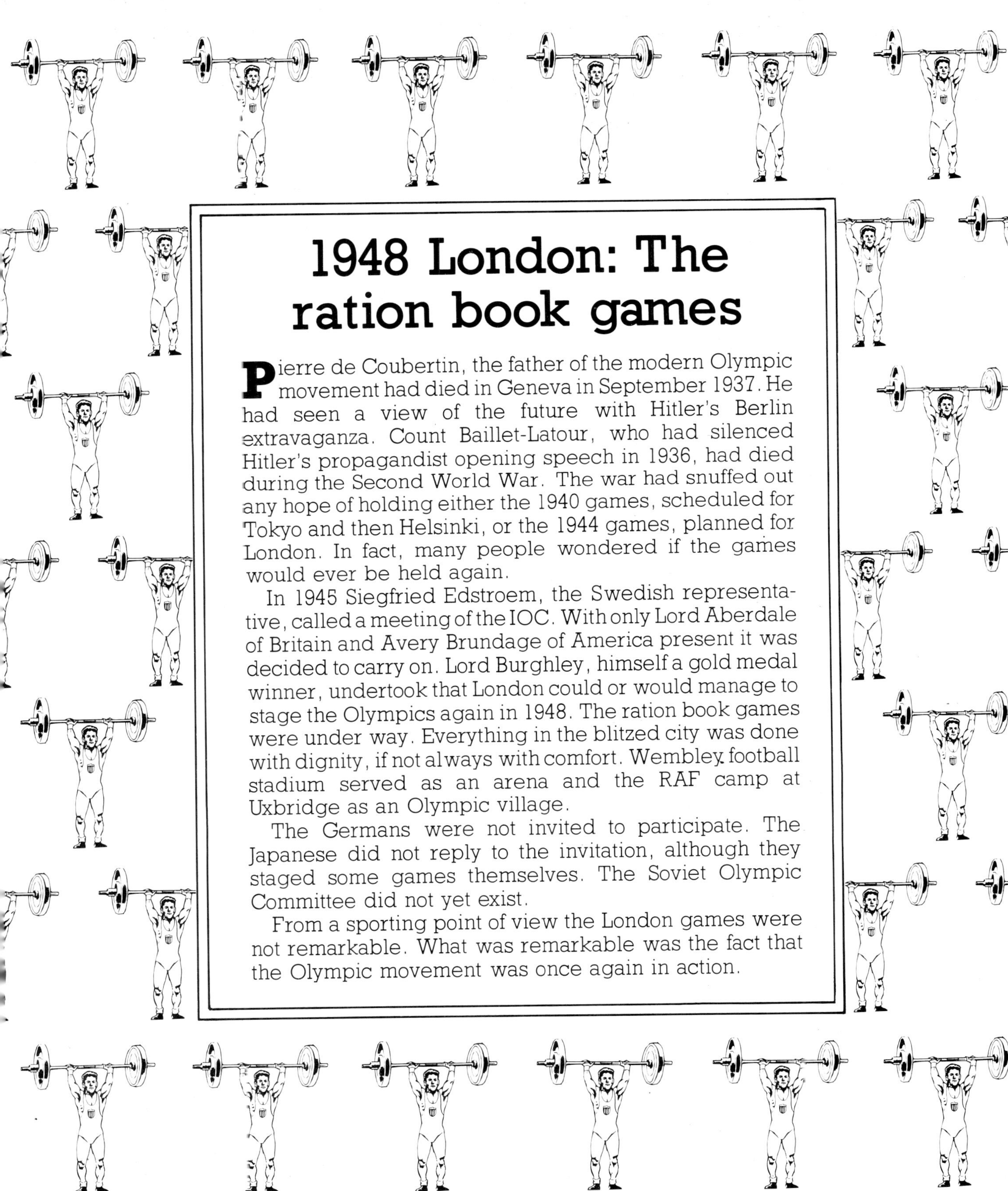

1948 London: The ration book games

Pierre de Coubertin, the father of the modern Olympic movement had died in Geneva in September 1937. He had seen a view of the future with Hitler's Berlin extravaganza. Count Baillet-Latour, who had silenced Hitler's propagandist opening speech in 1936, had died during the Second World War. The war had snuffed out any hope of holding either the 1940 games, scheduled for Tokyo and then Helsinki, or the 1944 games, planned for London. In fact, many people wondered if the games would ever be held again.

In 1945 Siegfried Edstroem, the Swedish representative, called a meeting of the IOC. With only Lord Aberdale of Britain and Avery Brundage of America present it was decided to carry on. Lord Burghley, himself a gold medal winner, undertook that London could or would manage to stage the Olympics again in 1948. The ration book games were under way. Everything in the blitzed city was done with dignity, if not always with comfort. Wembley football stadium served as an arena and the RAF camp at Uxbridge as an Olympic village.

The Germans were not invited to participate. The Japanese did not reply to the invitation, although they staged some games themselves. The Soviet Olympic Committee did not yet exist.

From a sporting point of view the London games were not remarkable. What was remarkable was the fact that the Olympic movement was once again in action.

1948: London: Make do and mend

In October 1945 Lord Burghley (later to become the Marquess of Exeter) flew to Stockholm to tell the IOC that London was prepared to stage the next games. The Second World War had finished less than three months earlier and the entire Olympic movement was wondering if the games would ever be held again.

The age of austerity

London's offer to hold the 1948 games was accepted. Preparations for the ration book games began. Everything was in short supply: food and clothing were on ration; prefabricated homes stood on bomb sites; coal for fuel, wood and steel for construction were scarce. The Allied victory had brought little to the British save shortages and hardship.

In the heatwave summer of 1948 there were doubts about London's ability to put on the games, yet they ended with acclaim all round. True, the athletes did not like being billetted at RAF Uxbridge, or even in the colleges at Richmond and Wimbledon. But in the make do and mend postwar atmosphere, athletes and officials knew what Britain and the rest of Europe had gone through, and everybody made allowance for shortcomings.

King George opened the games at England's soccer stadium, Wembley, on July 29. The banners of 59 nations were in the march past. Absent were Germany and Japan.

The Czech locomotive

Hardly had the games begun, when a new Olympic hero was born — Emil Zatopek. This lieutenant in the Czech army was unknown to a large degree, but in the 10,000m he literally ran his opponents off their legs to win in 29mins 59.6sec, with the nearest man, Alain Mimoun of France three quarters of a lap behind. Zatopek had run the final lap in 66 seconds.

His ungainly style, with his head pressed against his left shoulder, was something new to athletics. His training was also new. Zatopek ran ten miles and more every day in the hilly woods outside Prague. He believed stamina was the greatest asset in distance running — and nobody could prove him wrong.

Hero of Wembley

Zatopek, the instant hero of Wembley, brought a new training dimension to the sport. It has been modified and improved by others since. But the original theory belonged to this likeable Czech, who went on to take the silver medal in a mud-splattered 5,000m, behind the Belgian, Gaston Rieff. Zatopek was to reach the peak of his Olympic career in Helsinki.

In the 10,000m Zatopek ran a final lap of 66sec, leaving the next competitor almost 300m behind.

Conditions in London were far from comfortable immediately after the war, with athletes billeted in ex-army barracks. Emil Zatopek became the instant hero of the 1948 games. In the 5,000m he came second to Rieff (Belgium).

Top right: The Olympic motto and torch bearer in London, 1948, reviving the Olympic spirit after the Second World War.

Bottom: In lane one, the Flying Dutchwoman Fanny Blankers-Koen, on her way to the hurdles gold medal in London.

1948 London: Flying Dutchwoman and Jamaican jets

While Zatopek was the hero, there was no doubting who was the heroine of the 1948 games. Fanny Blankers-Koen had been coached by her husband in secret during the war in occupied Holland. She dominated the women's athletics with four gold medals. The Dutch, of course, were tremendously popular in London for their spirited resistance to the Germans and there was hardly a dry eye at Wembley when the Dutch anthem was played.

In three events Fanny prevented British gold medals. Yet even this failed to stop her support from the packed stadium. She won the 100m, 200m and 80m hurdles from Dorothy Manley, Audrey Williamson and Maureen Gardner.

Then the Flying Dutchwoman capped an astonishing games by helping Holland to victory in the relay at the expense of Australia. She was then 30 years of age and had competed in Berlin 12 years before.

But to Londoners there was something special about the 400m. Two great Jamaicans were lined up for battle — Arthur Wint and Herb McKenley. Wint belonged to London Polytechnic Harriers and at the time was more a Londoner than a West Indian.

McKenley, the favourite, had studied at US universities and had a pedigree of American races behind him.

McKenley bolted away at the gun, passed the 200m mark inside 21sec and was four metres up on Wint. The gap remained the same into the home stretch, but then Wint opened up and sped down the track, for victory in 46.2sec with daylight between him and McKenley. A marvellous race that is still recalled by many.

Champion at seventeen

Another great champion is Bob Mathias of America who, at 17, won that toughest of all competitions, the decathlon. He had been discus throwing and pole vaulting for only seven months.

The Jamaican jets Wint and McKenley lined up for the 400m. Wint had trained in London, McKenley in the USA. The local crowd backed Wint, who won.

Fanny Blankers-Koen was the heroine of the games. During the war she had trained in secret. Now she won four golds for Holland.

Bob Mathias (USA) won the decathlon at 17. His family came to look after him.

1948 London: Hot competition in hot weather

The 1948 100m was another great story. Harrison Dillard was the top high hurdler in America, but he failed to reach the US trials final in this event. So he switched to the 100m and qualified for Wembley. The race was billed as usual as a contest between the fastest men on earth. Lloyd La Beach of Panama was hot favourite.

Two Britons, McDonald Bailey (a West Indian who had served in the RAF and was with Poly, like Wint) and Alistair McCorquodale, both reached the final. But it was Dillard the hurdler, with an Olympic record of 10.3sec, who led the field home. Four years later he was to win his own speciality in Helsinki. La Beach took the bronze, as he did in the 200m when he found Mel Patton (USA) too hot for him.

Last lap marathon

As ever, the marathon produced thrills with the Frenchman, Etienne Gailly, running with controlled brilliance until within sight of Wembley's twin towers. Then the Argentinian, Delfo Cabrera sprang into the lead. Gailly struggled round the track but the Welshman Tom Richards, grey headed and wiry, found enough stamina to snatch even the silver from the gallant Frenchman's grasp.

Two boxers who were to make big names for themselves subsequently, began their careers at Wembley. The flyweight title went to the nuggety Argentinian, Pascual Perez. He was destined to dominate his weight in the professional ranks for many years. And at middleweight, Laszlo Papp of Hungary won the first of his three Olympic golds. He was to become the first professional sportsman from an Iron Curtain country.

Heatwave and polio

The heatwave summer of 1948 was brought, some said, by the Australian cricket team under Donald Bradman. Unfortunately the hot weather also brought a severe outbreak of polio, which struck the games. Eliska Miskova, a Czech gymnast, contracted the disease. She died three days later while her team-mates were in competition. That was the only sad moment of the games which turned out to be a great success and gave Britain a long-needed morale boost.

In the marathon Gailly (Fr) looked a winner, but within sight of Wembley he was passed by Cabrera (Arg) and Richards (GB).

Dillard (USA) failed to qualify for his event, the hurdles, so he entered the 100m.

DILLARD
BAILEY
McCORQUODALE
LA BEACH
EWELL
PATTON

La Beach was favourite, but Dillard was too fast for the 100m experts.

Records and results 1948

Shooter changes hands

Karoly Takacs of Hungary had been world champion in rapid fire pistol before World War II. In 1938 he lost his right hand, and took up shooting with his left. In 1948 and 1952 he won gold medals shooting left handed.

1948
1. K. Takacs (Hungary) 580pts.
2. C. Valiente (Argentina) 571pts.
3. S. Lundquist (Sweden) 569pts.

1952
1. K. Takacs (Hungary) 578pts.
2. S. Kun (Hungary) 578pts.
3. G. Lichiardopol (Rumania) 575pts.

Fabulous Fanny

Fanny Blankers-Koen, trained in secret by her husband in German-occupied Holland, became the outstanding woman athlete of 1948. At one time she held seven world records: 100yds, 220yds, 200m, 80m hurdles, high jump, long jump, pentathlon. These are her 1948 Olympic results:

	Heat	**semi-final**	**final**
100m	winner, 12sec	winner, 12sec	winner, 11.9sec
200m	winner, 25.7sec	winner, 24.3sec	winner 24.4sec
80m hurdles	winner, 11.3sec	winner, 11.4sec	winner, 11.2sec
4 x 100m relay	winner, 42.6sec		winner, 47.5sec

The Kayak King

Gert Fredriksson of Sweden is one of the unsung Olympic heroes, whose achievements seldom come to public notice. Here are his results:

1948 Kayak singles
1. G. Fredriksson (Sweden) 4mins 32.2sec
2. J. Andersen (Denmark)
3. H. Eberhardt (France)

1952 Kayak singles
1. G. Fredriksson (Sweden) 4mins 07.9sec
2. T. Stromberg (Finland)
3. L. Gantois (France)

1956 Kayak singles
1. G. Fredriksson (Sweden) 4mins 12.8sec
2. I. Pisarev (USSR)
3. L. Kiss (Hungary)

1960 Kayak doubles
1. Sweden 3mins 34.73sec
2. Hungary
3. Poland

Boxing — where the honours went

Some nations excel at certain events, and in boxing there is no doubt that the USA is the dominating influence. Surprisingly Britain ranks second with the USSR. Italy is close behind.

	Light flyweight	Fly-weight	Bantam weight	Feather-weight	Light-weight	Light welter-weight	Welter-weight	Light middle-weight	Middle weight		Heavy-weight	No of titles
1904	—	USA	USA	USA	USA	—	USA	—	USA	USA		7
1908	—	—	GB	GB	GB	—	—	—	GB	—	GB	5
1920	—	USA	S. Africa	France	USA	—	Canada	—	GB	—	GB	7
1924	—	USA	S. Africa	USA	Denmark	—	Belgium	—	GB	GB	Norway	8
1928	—	Hungary	Italy	Holland	Italy	—	NZ	—	Italy	Argentina	Argentina	8
1932	—	Hungary	Canada	Argentina	S.Africa	—	USA	—	USA	S. Africa	Argentina	8
1936	—	Germany	Italy	Argentina	Hungary	—	Finland	—	France	France	Germany	8
1948	—	Argentina	Hungary	Italy	S. Africa	—	Czech.	—	Hungary	S. Africa	Argentina	8
1952	—	USA	Finland	Czech.	Italy	USA	Poland	Hungary	USA	USA	USA	10
1956	—	GB	Germany	USSR	GB	USSR	Rumania	Hungary	USSR	USA	USA	10
1960	—	Hungary	USSR	Italy	Poland	Czech.	Italy	USA	USA	USA	Italy	10
1964	—	Italy	Japan	USSR	Poland	Poland	Poland	USSR	USSR	Italy	USA	10
1968	Venezuela	Mexico	USSR	Mexico	USA	Poland	E.Germany	USSR	GB	USSR	USA	11
1972	Hungary	Bulgaria	Cuba	USSR	Poland	USA	Cuba	W.Germany	USSR	Yugoslavia	Cuba	11
1976	Cuba	USA	N.Korea	Cuba	USA	USA	E.Germany	Poland	USA	USA	Cuba	11

USA	32	Argentina	7	Italy	11	East & West Germany	6
GB	12	Cuba	6	Hungary	9	In 1956, 60 and 64 East and	
USSR	12	South Africa	6	Poland	8	West Germany combined.	

Top right: Emil Zatopek, in thirteenth position, looks for an escape route in the 10,000m, which he won at Wembley in 1948.

Bottom left: The Dutch diver, Miss Floor, brought grace to the 1948 springboard competition.

Bottom right: Kuts (USSR) and Pirie (GB) faced each other in two epic battles in Melbourne in 1956. Kuts won both 5,000m and 10,000m golds.

Left: Harry Llewellyn and Foxhunter, winners of Britain's only gold medal in Helsinki, 1952.

Below: Uesako (Japan) competing in the 1952 men's gymnastics.

1952 Helsinki: City of athletic harmony

For once an Olympiad without any particular political or commercial cloud over it. Those who competed in and attended the Helsinki games still remember the sporting atmosphere and consider them to have been one of the most successful ever. They attracted more competitors than Melbourne or Rome, and as many as Tokyo in 1964.

For the Finns the honour of holding the games was well deserved. Finnish athletes had made their first appearance at Stockholm in 1912. This was the start of their 20-year domination of middle distance running. They also excelled in other sports — wrestling, javelin and gymnastics.

Helsinki had secured the games in competition with many other cities like Detroit, Minneapolis, Amsterdam, Chicago and Philadelphia. But the 5,876 athletes who took part appreciated the Finnish city for staging the games with simplicity, friendship and sportsmanship. Perhaps content with this, the Finns took few golds, in contrast to their pre-war performances.

1952 Helsinki: The Zatopeks, a four gold family

Outside the ultra modern stadium in Helsinki stands the statue of Paavi Nurmi. It served as a constant reminder to the IOC, which had banned him for professionalism — a rebuff reiterated when Nurmi strode into the stadium with the Olympic torch. And it served as an example to the distance runners of the world — and Nurmi's legend was to be challenged at Helsinki by one of the greatest of these, Emil Zatopek.

Zatopek's impossible triple

Now the Galloping Major of the Czech army, Zatopek set about the record book with a unique and totally unexpected triple. It was so unexpected that even he thought it was impossible!

As in London, Zatopek took the 10,000m with Alain Mimoun of France again second. The same two came first and second in the 5,000m. Zatopek had been clear winner on both occasions. It was then decided that the Galloping Major would try for the marathon.

The British favourite

The favourite was the British runner Jim Peters. During a delay at London Airport, while a senior British official gave a press interview, the team had been left sitting in the 'plane. Peters was in a draught which led to a chill. His illness was kept secret in the British camp and by the day of the marathon he was almost fully fit.

He began well, and nearing the halfway mark was joined by Zatopek, the novice in the race. Zatopek turned to Peters and asked if he thought they were going fast enough. 'I was amazed by his coolness and the next thing I knew he was racing away from me,' said Peters afterwards.

Whether Zatopek was using psychological tactics, or was merely curious will never be known. What is known is that the question shattered Peters' confidence.

Zatopek won and, as his wife Dana had won the javelin, they went home to Prague with four gold medals and the affection of the world.

There may have been 69 nations taking part, but Helsinki belonged to one man.

Zatopek was the hero of '52. He won the 10,000m easily. In the 5,000m final Chattaway (GB) led on the last bend. But in an instant he fell and was passed by Zatopek, Mimoun (Fr) and Schade (Germany).

Zatopek, the Czech Galloping Major, ran the marathon for the first time in his life and won the gold medal. His wife won the javelin gold. They went home a four gold family.

1952 Helsinki: Olympic record at the first attempt

Once again dedication to training and the ability to push himself through the walls of his own limitations on the lonely wooded hillsides had paid off for Zatopek. He ran alone for more than half the marathon. After leaving Peters there was no one ahead except the officials at the finish. He broke the Olympic record by six minutes with a time of 2hrs 23mins 3.2sec and immediately waved to the crowd and chatted with reporters. It was as though he had jogged a few metres to catch a bus. Never had the Olympic games seen such a winner of the marathon. 'I had to win this one,' he joked afterwards. 'The family score in golds was only 2-1 to me. Now it's 3-1'.

Disappointing debut

Zatopek had stolen the glitter from the vast Russian team that made its post-war re-appearance at the games. The rest of the world had heard of the magnificent training times of Soviet athletes and the Americans, in particular, had expected a serious assault on their Olympic domination.

But in the men's track events the Russians could muster only two silvers, one by Vladimir Kazantsev in the steeplechase, and the other by Juri Lituev in the 400m hurdles, plus a bronze in the 10,000m by Alexandr Anufriev. Their only gold medal came in the 10km walk in which Junk led the field home.

Jamaican relay

Herb McKenley, now running for London Polytechnic Harriers, again took the silver in the 400m, behind another Jamaican, George Rhoden, and Arthur Wint was second to Mal Whitfield (USA) in the 800m. Whitfield had also won the title in London, four years earlier, with Wint second.

Then McKenley, Rhoden and Wint, plus Les Laing making up the Jamaican team shattered the world record in the 4 x 400m relay. But they beat the USA by only one metre.

Old at twenty-one?

Bob Mathias won the decathlon again at the ripe old age of 21! Three Russian girls graced the podium after the discus — a clear pointer to the Soviet Olympic future.

Parry O'Brien brought a new technique to the shot. O'Brien developed the modern halfturn, bringing with it greater lift and force. He won the gold (and defended it in Melbourne) with a heave of 17m 41cm.

Emil Zatopek's dedicated training won him a marathon gold in a record time of 2hrs 23mins 3.2sec.

During the marathon Zatopek cooled off after 30kms by lifting his vest.

Parry O'Brien developed a new shot technique, the modern half-turn, and won the gold with a throw of 17m 41cm.

1952 Helsinki: A foretaste of boxing's finest

They were both heavyweight champions, but they had conflicting upbringings and contrasting fortunes at the games. Floyd Patterson was the coloured boy from the wrong side of the tracks. At 17 years of age Patterson, from the harsh world of Brooklyn, was overseas for the first time. In pre-fight training he impressed reporters with his quietly-spoken courtesy. He was not shy, and for his years, he handled interviews with great panache, which was to stay with him throughout his long career.

In the ring only one of his four opponents went the distance with him. His speed and hammer right were too much for them. He was outstanding in the middleweight class — a fact illustrated by his 74 seconds knock-out win over Vasile Tita (Rumania) in the final.

Gentleman boxer

By contrast the Swedish heavyweight, Ingemar Johansson, had come from middle class stock, was at ease in any company, exuded self confidence and was disqualified in the final for not trying. No silver medal was awarded.

Johansson faced the 19 year-old US sailor, Eddie Sanders, who had won his three preliminary fights inside the distance. He was clear favourite and Johansson knew all about the American's lethal punch.

Boring performance

The Swede danced through the first round out of range with the crowd booing his boring performance. The second round continued in the same way with Sanders often looking at the referee in disbelief. In the end the referee called a halt and Sanders had won by that strange boxing verdict, a walk-over.

It took years for Johansson to live down that embarrassing moment. He later took the world heavyweight crown from Floyd Patterson. But the boy from Brooklyn regained it. Both men were respected for their sportsmanship and ability in the professional ring.

Laszlo Papp, of Hungary, won a second gold medal when he took the light middleweight crown on points from the South African, Theus van Schalkwyk. Papp went on to become European middleweight professional champion in 1962.

Floyd Patterson (USA) at 17 proved himself master of the middleweight class. In the final he knocked out Tita (Rumania) in 74sec.

Papp (Hungary) took the light middleweight gold, defeating van Schalkwyk (S. Africa) on points. Papp went on to be the first East European professional.

Johansson (Sweden) was disqualified in the final of the heavyweight competition for not trying against Sanders (USA).

1952 Helsinki: A horse saves Britain's honour

Bannister had failed in the 1,500m; Chataway and Pirie in the 5,000m; Pirie, Sando and Norris in the 10,000m; Peters in the marathon, Disley in the steeplechase. Who could turn the tide for Britain on the final day?

Colonel Llewellyn and his horse Foxhunter won Britain's only gold in Helsinki. Elvestroem of Denmark dominated the sailing events and the world saw for the first time the awesome talent of the Hungarian football team.

The hero, a horse

Not a man, not a woman, but a horse! The British were lying seventh in the team event, the Prix des Nations. Col. Harry Llewellyn was riding Foxhunter and they needed a clear round to put Britain in with a chance. Foxhunter was magnificent. He leapt every obstacle with plenty to spare and his clear round took the team into the gold medal position ahead of Chile and the United States. Incidentally that round was good enough to secure Foxhunter only 15th spot in the individual placings. But he did win that most important of all battles — the final one!

Sailing away

The Dane, Peter Elvestroem was busy winning the Finn Class in the yachting, to add to his gold medal in 1948. He won four races out of six to win the title in a canter. He was to get two more golds, in 1956 and 1960, to prove how great an Olympic sailor he was. He is now world famous as a sailmaker.

Magical Magyars

And on the subject of greatness, Helsinki saw the birth of one of the greatest of all soccer machines — the Hungarians — later to beat England 6-3 at Wembley and 7-1 in Budapest.

In the 1952 Olympics they beat Yugoslavia 2-0 in the final. The magical Magyars scored 20 goals in five games with a poetic performance that stamped them as an all-time great side. In goal was Grosits; Lantos at left back, Lorant at centre-half, and centre-forward Palotis, all were stars.

But the deep lying Hidegkuti, inside right Kocsis and left wing Czibor were constellations. And shining above all was the legendary Ferenc Puskas, later to lead Real Madrid to some of their best wins. Two years after the Olympics Hungary somehow lost the World Cup final 3-2 to West Germany.

The 1956 Hungarian Revolution saw the team break up. But Helsinki witnessed in 1952 a new kind of football that was to change the game for ever.

Records and Results: 1952

Zatopek — the distance triple

Only Emil Zatopek of Czechoslovakia would have attempted anything so amazing as three golds at 5,000m, 10,000m and marathon. And he did it! This is how:

20.7.52
10,000m
1. E. Zatopek (Czech.) 29mins 17sec new world record
2. A Mimoun (France)
3. A. Anufriev (USSR)

24.7.52
5,000m
1. E. Zatopek (Czech.) 14mins 06.6sec new Olympic record
2. A. Mimoun (France)
3. H. Schade (Germany)

27.4.52
Marathon
1. E. Zatopek (Czech.) 2hrs 23mins 03.2sec new Olympic record
2. S. Gorno (Argentina)
3. G. Jansson (Sweden)

The Magical Magyars

Football as an Olympic sport has been the subject of almost endless dispute about professionalism. What has never been disputed is that the Hungarians of the 1950s (professional or not, they were mostly army personnel) brought a new light to the game. This is the Hungarian line-up, which won the 1952 Olympic championship against Yugoslavia. The goals were by Puskas (70min) and Csibor (88min).

Gyula Grosics

Mihaly Lantos — Jeno Buzansky

Jozsef Bozsik — Gyula Lorant — Jozsef Zakarias

Nandor Hidegkuti — Zoltan Csibor

Sandor Kocsis — Ferenc Puskas

Peter Palotas

Men's gymnastics: Japan v USSR

Two nations have consistently battled for supremacy in the men's gymnastics, Japan and Russia. Here are the results of each games from 1952-1976. To date the Russians have won 24 golds and the Japanese 19.

Event	1952	1956	1960	1964	1968	1972	1976
Combined exercises	USSR	USSR	USSR	Japan	Japan	Japan	USSR
Floor Exercises	Sweden	USSR	Japan	Italy	Japan	USSR	USSR
Pommelled Horse	USSR	USSR	USSR Finland	Yugoslavia	Yugoslavia	USSR	Hungary
Rings	USSR	USSR	USSR	Japan	Japan	Japan	USSR
Vault	USSR	USSR Germany	USSR Japan	Japan	USSR	E. Germany	USSR
Parallel Bars	Switzerland	USSR	USSR	Japan	Japan	Japan	Japan
Horizontal Bars	Switzerland	Japan	Japan	USSR	USSR Japan	Japan	Japan

Sweden's pentathlon record

Between 1912 and 1952 Sweden only once failed to take the modern pentathlon gold. Since 1952 Hungary has taken three golds, Sweden two and Poland one.

1912	Gustav Lillehook	(Sweden)
1920	Gustav Dryssen	(Sweden)
1924	Bo Lindman	(Sweden)
1928	Sven Thofelt	(Sweden)
1932	J.G. Oxenstierna	(Sweden)
1936	Gotthard Handrick	(Germany)
1948	Willi Grut	(Sweden)
1952	Lars Hall	(Sweden)

1952 medal table

Country	Gold	Silver	Bronze
USA	40	19	17
USSR	22	30	17
Hungary	16	10	16
Sweden	12	13	10
Italy	8	9	4
Czech.	7	3	3
France	6	6	6
Australia	6	2	3
Finland	4	6	3
Norway	3	2	0
Switz.	2	6	6
S. Africa	2	4	3
Denmark	2	1	3
Jamaica	2	3	-
Belgium	2	2	-
Turkey	2	-	1
Japan	1	6	2
Britain	1	2	8
Argentina	1	2	2
Poland	1	2	1
Rumania	1	1	2
Canada	1	2	-
Yugoslavia	1	2	-
Brazil	1	-	2
NZ	1	-	2
India	1	-	1
Luxemburg	1	-	-

Top left: Paavo Nurmi, disqualified from the games of 1932 because of alleged professionalism, was still the hero of Finland 20 years later when he lit the flame at Helsinki.

Top right: Bob Mathias in pole-vault action during the decathlon which he won in 1948 and 1952.

Left: A family celebration in in the pool at Helsinki following the victory of the Frenchman Boiteux in the 400m. Father jumped in to congratulate his son.

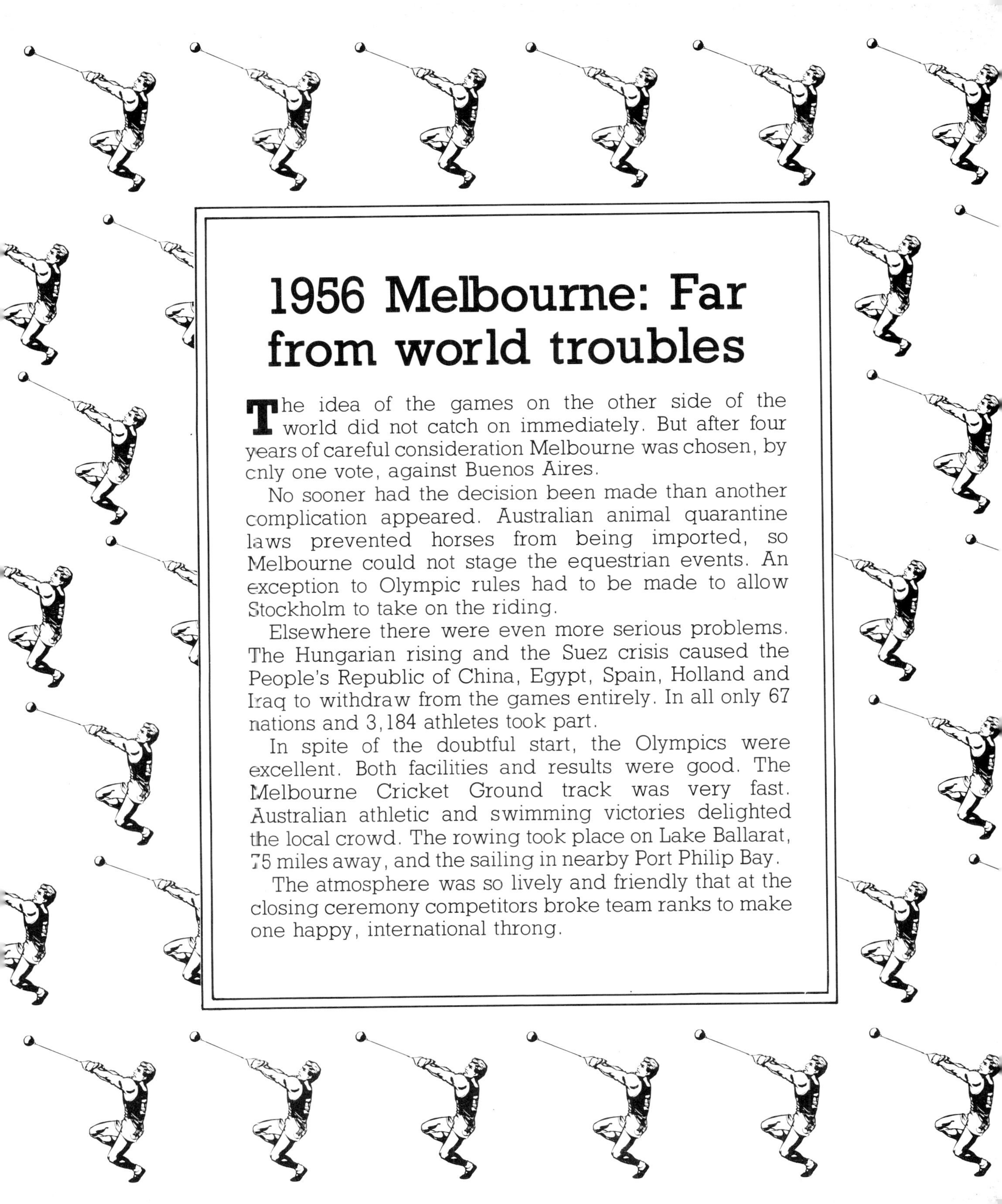

1956 Melbourne: Far from world troubles

The idea of the games on the other side of the world did not catch on immediately. But after four years of careful consideration Melbourne was chosen, by only one vote, against Buenos Aires.

No sooner had the decision been made than another complication appeared. Australian animal quarantine laws prevented horses from being imported, so Melbourne could not stage the equestrian events. An exception to Olympic rules had to be made to allow Stockholm to take on the riding.

Elsewhere there were even more serious problems. The Hungarian rising and the Suez crisis caused the People's Republic of China, Egypt, Spain, Holland and Iraq to withdraw from the games entirely. In all only 67 nations and 3,184 athletes took part.

In spite of the doubtful start, the Olympics were excellent. Both facilities and results were good. The Melbourne Cricket Ground track was very fast. Australian athletic and swimming victories delighted the local crowd. The rowing took place on Lake Ballarat, 75 miles away, and the sailing in nearby Port Philip Bay.

The atmosphere was so lively and friendly that at the closing ceremony competitors broke team ranks to make one happy, international throng.

1956 Melbourne: Double challenge, double victory

Once again the Olympics were to open in 1956 to the distant rumble of war. Russian tanks were in the streets of Budapest and the Anglo-French forces had landed in Suez. As a result the Dutch, Egyptian and Spanish teams withdrew from the games in protest. Half the Hungarian team reached Australia, the other half flew home from Singapore As in previous Olympiads the spirit of the games had been clouded by bitterness and inhumanity.

The IOC also had its problems because of the Australian quarantine laws the equestrian events had to be held in Stockholm.

event. The Russian opened with a fierce lap of 61.4sec. Pirie was still there and in control. Lap after lap the red vest went metre for metre with the all-white strip of Britain.

Kuts kept accelerating in long bursts, but could not shake off the Englishman. In the 20th lap Pirie surged ahead and the fans held their breath. But then, as if punctured, Pirie cracked. Suddenly it was over. Kuts ran home alone in 28mins 45.6sec, nearly 90sec faster than Zatopek's Olympic record.

The second meeting

The 5,000m was almost an anti-climax. Pirie could not chase his

Discord in the IOC.

Kuts (USSR) and Pirie (GB), giants of the 5,000 and 10,000metres.

Kuts' tactics of constant accelerations broke Pirie's resistance in the 10,000m.

First race, first clash

But once the athletics started world attention was rivetted on two men, Vladimir Kuts, the Russian sailor, and Gordon Pirie the Surrey bank clerk. Each saw the other as his main rival. And Kuts, the 1954 European champion, still remembered his defeat by Britain's Chris Chataway at the White City two years before. From this developed a respect for English runners that was to prove his greatest asset.

The first clash came after the opening ceremony with the 10,000m man a second time. Although the British bank clerk held the world record, he let Kuts run his own race. And at the end the Russian had eleven seconds in hand, again slashing the Olympic record of Zatopek. Pirie ran in for his silver medal followed a few steps behind by his countryman Derek Ibbotson.

Twice Kuts had broken away from the field. In the 5,000m he would surely have beaten the world record had there been someone to challenge him over the last 1,000 metres. He was 2.8sec outside Pirie's mark.

In the 5,000m Kuts took the gold and a new Olympic record.

1956 Melbourne: East-West love and hate

The Hungarians in the Olympic Village never really knew what was happening in Budapest. Throughout the games they worried about the fate of their families and friends. So, when Hungary met the Soviet Union at water polo bitter feeling erupted.

Water polo, not war

The Hungarians were giving their rivals a lesson in the sport. Then a Russian fist split Zador's eye and the clear pool was streaked with blood. The Hungarians reacted immediately and the Russians were pummelled into a corner of the pool by a storm of flailing arms and fists.

Fighting broke out among spectators, the police were called in. Eventually order was restored and the Hungarians won 4-0, going on to take the gold medals.

When the Russian team went up to collect their bronze medals they had a noticeably cool reception from the Hungarians and Yugoslav silver medallists.

A win disputed

The world record-holder for the steeplechase was the Hungarian, Rozsnyoi but he ran eight seconds slower than his best in the final, in which the unexpected victor was Chris Brasher of Britain Brasher had never won a major event and retired with his gold.

But it was three hours before he could collect his medal! He had been disqualified. Judges said he had interfered with the race on the final lap, when he edged into the lead between Rozsnyoi and the Norwegian, Larson. Rozsnyoi was announced the winner, but Brasher took his case to the Jury of Appeal, which upheld him on the grounds that there was no 'wilful' obstruction. So the title was his in 8mins 41.2sec, six seconds faster than he'd ever run before!

East loves West

In the end the East-West confrontations on and off the field of sport were not all shrouded in bitterness. Two people fell in love and even the Iron Curtain could not keep them apart. Hal Connolly, a 25 year-old, good-looking American, won the hammer title with his fifth throw of 63m 19cm. But more important to him, he won the heart of the discus champion, Olga Fikotova. The couple were married and left the games symbolising happiness and warmth — the very ideals of the Olympics!

Bitter feelings erupted in the water polo between Russia and Hungary, because of the Russian invasion. Brasher (GB) was disqualified in the steeplechase, and had to take his case to the Jury of Appeal before he was allowed a gold medal.

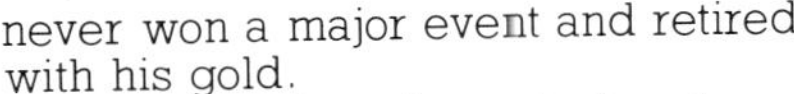

Connolly (US) won the hammer gold and the heart of discus champion Fikotova (Czech.)

1956 Melbourne: Local girl makes good three golds

It's always satisfying to see local competitors doing well in the games, and the Australian fans certainly had their share of successes. The uncrowned queen of the games was blonde teenager, Betty Cuthbert. She won three gold medals for sprinting, and surprised even the Australians with her performance. They had expected Marlene Mathews to be their No 1 in the 100m and 200m.

In the 100m, Betty, with an explosive start and good pick-up, had two metres to spare. But it took the camera to decide between the German Christa Stubnick and Miss Mathews.

The 18 year-old Sydney girl again gave her rivals a clean pair of heels in the 200m, which she won in 23.4sec. Mathews was drawn in lane one with Cuthbert in lane five and Stubnick on the outside. Both Cuthbert and Stubnick were therefore running blind. Cuthbert showed her immense finishing power to surge through the tape well clear of both rivals. The same three girls had taken the first three places in both 100m and 200m

British relay force

Although the British women sprinters had not done much individually, they were collectively a considerable relay force. In fact, they broke the world record with a time of 44.7sec. But this wasn't good enough.

Once again Betty Cuthbert stole the limelight with as perfect a piece of relay running as had ever been seen. For Britain June Paul handed over to Heather Armitage in first place, and with 50m remaining the English girl was still holding off Cuthbert's challenge. But again that powerful finish told. Australia won in 44.5sec and yet another Olympic heroine joined the ranks of the all time greats.

In their own special way the Australians went wild about her. The headline in a Melbourne paper screamed, 'You Beaut Cow Bet'!

A second local gold

The Australians had another ace to call upon in the 80m hurdles. Shirley Strickland had been eliminated early on in the 100m, but in her speciality she quickly showed the rest that she was there to defend the title she won in Helsinki. Shirley won her opening heat in 10.8sec, and repeated that time in the semi-finals. In this race she held off a late challenge by the German, Gisele Kohler, and the psychological impact of this was seen in the final. Against a headwind, the Australian gave one of the best hurdling performances seen at the games. She clocked 10.7sec, with Miss Kohler well back in second position. Norma Thrower came through for the bronze to make it gold and bronze for Australia.

Betty Cuthbert was the local hero, winning three gold medals, the 100m, the 200m and the 4 x 100m relay.

Shirley Strickland's speciality was the 80m hurdles. She successfully defended the title she won in Helsinki against Kohler (Germany) and Thrower (Australia).

1956 Melbourne: Australian domination in the swimming

Australian swimming came of age with a vengeance in Melbourne. Eight of the 13 titles were held Down Under. The Australians took all the medals in the men's and women's sprints; they won both relays and took gold and silver in two other events; and 17 year-old Murray Rose, born in Birmingham, brought up in Sydney, won the two most punishing events, the 400m and 1,500m.

Tactics for Breen

In the heats the American George Breen had set a world record of 17mins 52.9sec and was clearly the man to beat in the final. But Rose and the Japanese Takashi Yamanaka had the tactics for the race. Breen had his rivals on either side of him, and they set out to control his devastating opening.

For 800m Breen swam ahead of his challengers, but try as he might, he couldn't get away from them. Then at 850m Rose hit the front. Breen had nothing left, possibly because of his heat time and only Yamanaka was left to challenge. As in the 400m, he found the Australian's sprint finish too much and Rose won his second gold of the games in superlative style. He clocked 17mins 58.9sec.

Three Australian flags

Then there was the young Sydney girl, Dawn Fraser, 16 years of age, with a training background that would frighten a lot of men. Five hours a day she swam under her father's coaching, often in Sydney harbour. He believed swimming against waves and currents strengthened his daughter.

In the women's 100m final, Dawn proved the point by beating Lorraine Crapp and Faith Leech into the minor placings and three Australian flags went up at the victory ceremony. Miss Crapp avenged the defeat in the 400m. Then Fraser, Crapp, Leech and Sandra Morgan teamed up to win the relay.

The favourite wins

The men's 100m had seen outsiders winning in the previous three games, but the hot favourite, the Australian Jon Henricks, stopped the rot with victory over his team-mates Devitt and Chapman in 55.4sec.

Britain won her first swimming gold since 1924 when the London girl, Judy Grinham won the 100m backstroke in 72.9sec, with another Londoner, Margaret Edwards securing the bronze.

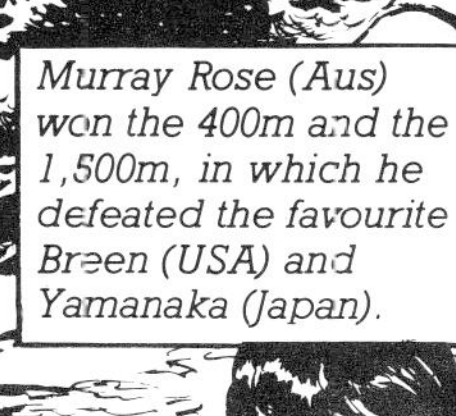

Murray Rose (Aus) won the 400m and the 1,500m, in which he defeated the favourite Breen (USA) and Yamanaka (Japan).

Australians took eight out of 13 swimming titles in Melbourne. Jon Henricks (Aus) was favourite and won the 100m ahead of team mates Devitt and Chapman in 55.4sec.

Dawn Fraser trained five hours a day – a regime which paid off with two golds and a silver.

1956 Melbourne: When Irish eyes are smiling

The crowd sang 'When Irish Eyes are Smiling'. The emerald-vested victor knelt and prayed. Ronnie Delaney, a 21 year-old Dubliner, whose loss of form almost kept him out of the games, came right on the night and won the 1,500m.

Everything before the race had pointed to the Englishman Ken Wood, the Australian John Landy, or the Hungarian Laszlo Tabori. Wood ran sensibly from the back, as the British tend to do, for two laps. He then found himself boxed in, but managed to extricate himself.

On the final lap everyone waited for the Yorkshireman's burst. But he ran straight into another box and it was Delaney who went charging past the pack on the outside of the home straight. Before anyone could react, the Irishman was beyond reach. It was a fine tactical race and the victory in 3mins 41.2sec, was just 0.6sec outside the world mark.

Out of the shadows

Alain Mimoun (France) had lived in Zatopek's shadow in 1948 and 1952. He now came into his own and won the marathon in 2hrs 25mins. The great Czech was still good enough to finish sixth.

The Norwegian Egil Danielsen won his country's first gold for 36 years in athletics. He did it in style with a world record 85m 71cm throw, more than two metres further than the previous javelin record.

In Melbourne, if they didn't know it already, pressmen found out just how hard it is to cover the games.

All were in bed after a long day when the lines from London started buzzing. Fencer Gillian Sheen had won the women's foil and the first anyone knew of it was when the international agency tapes were received in London. Next day most British papers carried stories about 'How I had breakfast with Gillian Sheen'. It must have been some meal! In fairness, it is impossible for two or three men from one newspaper to cover the Olympics fully.

Bulldog boxing

But they were all there for the boxing, which saw Terry Spinks win the flyweight and Dick McTaggart the lightweight. Dick also won the boxer of the games title. Seven British boxers came home with two golds, a silver and two bronzes.

Mimoun of France, having been in Zatopek's shadow for two Olympics, won the marathon. Zatopek was sixth.

Ron Delaney of Ireland was the surprise victor of the 1,500m. His tactics were perfect. After crossing the line he knelt and prayed.

Norwegian Danielsen won his country's first athletics gold for 36 years.

Terry Spinks and Dick McTaggart of Britain each took a boxing gold.

Records and results: 1956

Australia scoops the pool

Australian swimmers delighted the home crowds in Melbourne by taking eight out of 13 possible gold medals. These are the results:

Men's 100m freestyle
1. John Henricks (Australia) 55.4sec new Olympic record
2. John Devitt (Australia) 55.8sec
3. Gary Chapman (Australia) 56.7sec

Men's 400m freestyle
1. Murray Rose (Australia) 4mins 27.3sec new Olympic record
2. Tsuyoshi Yamanaka (Japan) 4mins 30.4sec
3. George Breen (USA) 4mins 32.5sec

Men's 1,500m freestyle
1. Murray Rose (Australia) 17min 58.9sec
2. Tsuyoshi Yamanaka (Japan) 18mins 00.3sec
3. George Breen (USA) 18mins 08.2sec

Men's 100m backstroke
1. David Thiele (Australia) 1min 02.2sec new Olympic record
2. John Monckton (Australia) 1min 03.2sec
3. Frank McKinney (USA) 1min 04.5sec

Men's 4 x 200m freestyle relay
1. Australia (O'Halloran, Devitt, Rose, Henricks) 8mins 23.6sec new world record
2. USA 8mins 31.5sec
3. USSR 8mins 34.7sec

Women's 100m freestyle
1. Dawn Fraser (Australia) 1min 02 sec new world record
2. Lorraine Crapp (Australia) 1min 02.3sec
3. Faith Leech (Australia) 1min 05.1sec

Women's 400m freestyle
1. Lorraine Crapp (Australia) 4mins 54.6sec new Olympic record
2. Dawn Fraser (Australia) 5mins 02.5sec
3. Sylvia Ruuska (USA) 5mins 07.1sec

Women's 4 x 100m freestyle relay
1. Australia (Fraser, Leech, Morgan, Crapp) 4mins 17.1sec new world record
2. USA 4mins 19.2sec
3. South Africa 4mins 25.7sec

Swimming medal table	Gold	Silver	Bronze
Australia	8	4	2
USA	2	4	6
Japan	1	4	-
Germany	1	-	1
Britain	1	-	-
Hungary	-	1	1
USSR	-	-	2
South Africa	-	-	1

Mimoun — Olympic bridesmaid

Algerian born Alain Mimoun of France waited eight years to win Olympic gold. He had the bad luck to meet Zatopek and take three silvers behind him in 1948 and 1952. In 1956 he beat Zatopek at last!

1948

10,000m
1. E. Zatopek (Czech.) 29mins 59.6sec
2. A. Mimoun (France) 30mins 47.4sec
3. D. Albertsson (Sweden) 30mins 53.6sec

1952

5,000m
1. E. Zatopek (Czech.) 14mins 06.6sec
2. A. Mimoun (France) 14mins 07.4sec
3. H. Schade (Germany) 14mins 08.6sec

10,000m
1. E. Zatopek (Czech.) 29mins 17sec
2. A. Mimoun (France) 29mins 32.8sec
3. A. Annfriev (USSR) 29mins 48.2sec

1956

Marathon
1. A. Mimoun (France) 2hrs 25mins
2. F. Milhalic (Yugoslavia) 2hrs 26mins 32sec
3. V. Karvonen (Finland) 2hrs 27mins 47sec
6. E. Zatopek (Czech.) 2hrs 29mins 34sec

Laszlo Papp, boxer supreme

Papp is the only man so far to win three consecutive times in Olympic boxing. He then became the only East European to turn professional.

1948

Middleweight
1. L. Papp (Hungary)
2. J. Wright (GB)
3. L. Fontana (Italy)

1952

Light middleweight
1. L. Papp (Hungary)
2. T. van Schalkwyk (S. Africa)
3. D. Tilshia (USSR)
   E. Herrera (Argentina)

1956

Light middleweight
1. L. Papp (Hungary)
2. J. Torres (USA)
3. J. McCormach (GB)
   Z. Pietrzykowski (Poland)

Papp went on to become European Middleweight Champion 1962-1964, winning seven championship fights until his travel permit was revoked by the Hungarian government and he had to return home.

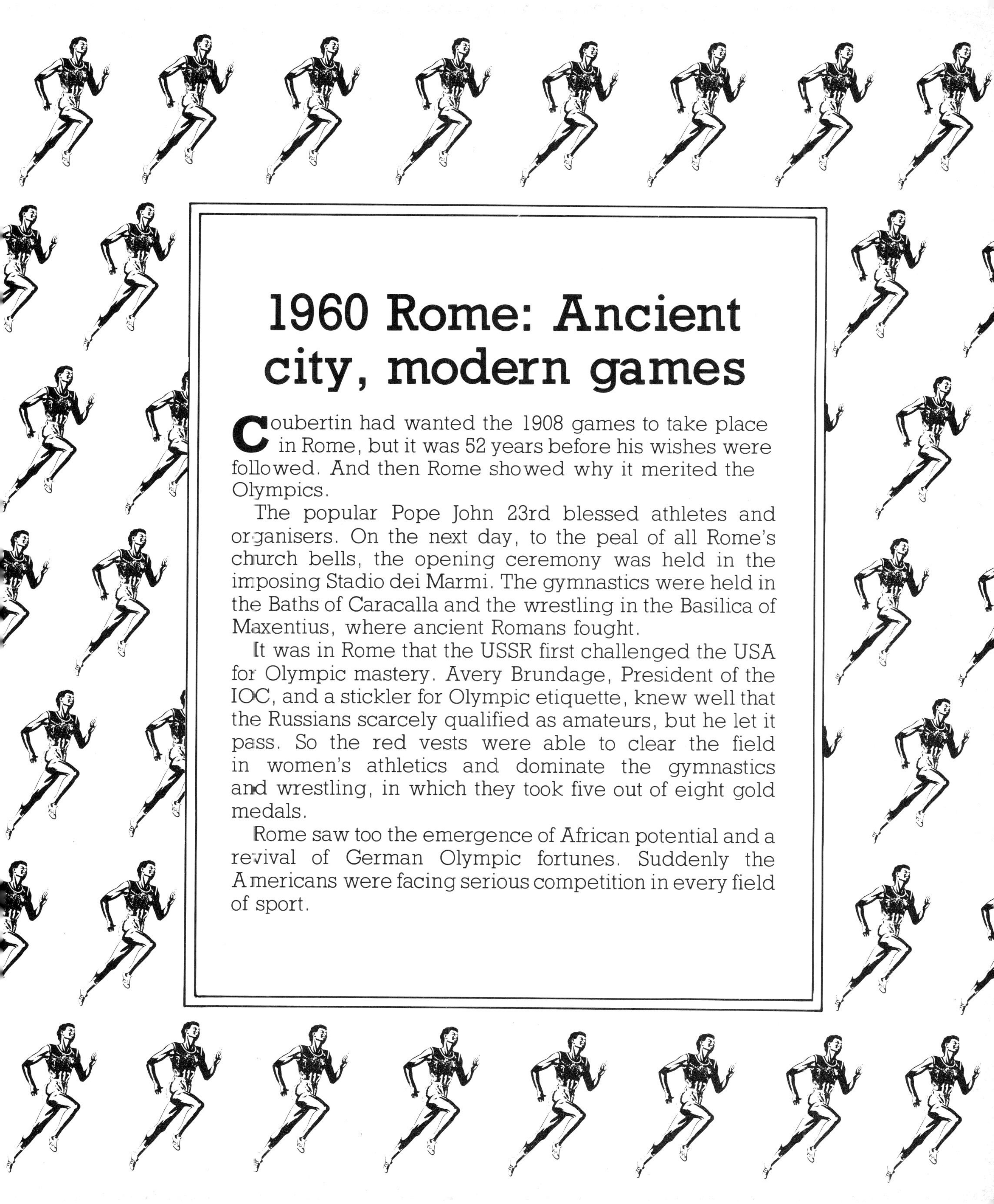

1960 Rome: Ancient city, modern games

Coubertin had wanted the 1908 games to take place in Rome, but it was 52 years before his wishes were followed. And then Rome showed why it merited the Olympics.

The popular Pope John 23rd blessed athletes and organisers. On the next day, to the peal of all Rome's church bells, the opening ceremony was held in the imposing Stadio dei Marmi. The gymnastics were held in the Baths of Caracalla and the wrestling in the Basilica of Maxentius, where ancient Romans fought.

It was in Rome that the USSR first challenged the USA for Olympic mastery. Avery Brundage, President of the IOC, and a stickler for Olympic etiquette, knew well that the Russians scarcely qualified as amateurs, but he let it pass. So the red vests were able to clear the field in women's athletics and dominate the gymnastics and wrestling, in which they took five out of eight gold medals.

Rome saw too the emergence of African potential and a revival of German Olympic fortunes. Suddenly the Americans were facing serious competition in every field of sport.

1960 Rome: Two great men on the road to Rome

Among those on the road to Rome, making their Olympic pilgrimage to the Eternal City, were two of the finest sportsmen the world has ever seen. One was a quietly spoken West Australian, Herb Elliott, already acknowledged as king of the mile and the other was a lesser known Louisville boxer, Cassius Marcellus Clay III.

The 1,500m final was probably one of the best races ever seen at the games. It rivalled the Lovelock race in Berlin, but for a totally different reason. Lovelock had challengers. Herb had none, so he took on the clock.

A poor field

On reflection it was a poor field. Elliott was so much better than the rest of the world that there was no contest. Had the East German, Sigi Valentin, not been injured before the games there might have been more of a race. As it was, Elliott gave a classic demonstration of middle-distance running that showed style, power and speed. He smashed the world record with a time of 3mins 35.6sec — a time that was to stand for years.

It was an elegant success and 0.4sec faster than Elliott's own best. Every one of the finalists turned out to cheer Elliott at the victory ceremony.

Not yet the greatest

Cassius Clay, later to become 'The Greatest', as he put it, won the light-heavyweight boxing crown. And it is strange, so long afterwards, to recall that many felt he was lucky to get a semi-final verdict over the tough Australian, Tony Madigan. He said at the time he had won and has maintained that standpoint through the years. Many experienced critics support Madigan's claim.

Nonetheless, Clay was on his way to super-stardom and who can deny that he may well have been the greatest professional heavyweight champion of them all.

It's one of sport's mysteries that it took a man like Cassius Clay-Muhammad Ali years to achieve similar pinnacles of excellence that the 22 year-old runner from Perth, scaled in less than four minutes.

Two great sportsmen were in action in Rome. Cassius Clay, later to become 'the greatest', and Herb Elliott, Australian 1,500m champion.

1960 Rome: New Zealand — two golds in 90 minutes

The small man in the black blazer with the silver fern on its breast pocket predicted confidently: 'We'll win two golds in 90 minutes and Sir Arthur Porritt will present the medals.'

Murray Halberg was certainly well fancied for the 5,000m. But who was the other New Zealander? 'Cometh the hour, cometh the man', said the man in the blazer, the New Zealand coach, Arthur Lydiard. 'You watch Peter Snell. The 800m is his.'

Cometh Peter Snell

At 20 Snell had experienced virtually no international competition. But this strong-legged Aucklander was made for success. He had basic speed, plus immense leg and shoulder power developed by Lydiard's revolutionary and extremely rigorous training programme.

Two men were favourites, the flowing West Indian George Kerr, and the Belgian policeman, Roger Moens, world record-holder. Snell tried out his tactics in the heats, breaking for home with 300 metres left, delaying the final surge.

He met Moens twice in the heats, losing first and then winning. In his eyes that left only Kerr. Still, few people rated Snell's chances as high. But in the final dash Moens and Kerr were so pre-occupied with each other that Snell was able to whip past both in his final strides to cross the line in 1min 46.3sec.

First love rugby

Also from Auckland was the man with the withered arm, Halberg. His first love was rugby but an arm injury put him out of that sport. So he took up running. Then came failure at Melbourne and again at Cardiff in the Commonwealth Games.

'After my defeat I stood there in the middle of the Temple of Welsh Rugby and saw myself as a total failure,' said Halberg. 'I wanted to quit, but felt it was worth maybe one more try.'

Out of range

So Halberg arrived in Rome. Lydiard was able to inspire him with belief in his ability. Halberg tore the field apart with a seering burst 1,000m from the tape, which left them all floundering. The East German, Hans Grodotzki and the Pole, Kazimierz Zimny, did narrow the gap before the end. But that lightning strike had put them 30 metres down and no one was going to catch Halberg from that range.

It was the day of the All Blacks. That small country had placed two more runners alongside Lovelock.

A year later, in Dublin, Halberg and Snell performed another amazing feat. Together with Barry Magee, who was to feature in the Rome marathon, and quarter-miler Gary Philpott, they broke the world 4 x 1 mile record — and not a miler amongst them at that stage!

Peter Snell was almost unknown when he won the 800m in Rome.

NZ coach Lydiard trained both Snell and Halberg.

Halberg won the 5,000m and then collapsed.

1960 Rome: The barefoot guard and the black gazelle

Once again the marathon produced a story of its own. This most famous of all Olympic races rarely fails to stir the imagination. It is an event that most people identify with because they just cannot imagine themselves running so far — 26miles 385 yards. It is the ultimate challenge, but to Abebe Bikila it must have seemed even more than that.

There he was in Italy, the country which had invaded his native Ethiopia in the 1930s. There he was having to run past the monument erected by Mussolini to the Italian soldiers, who died beating off brave tribesmen.

Four firsts for Bikila

His was to be the first gold medal won by an Ethiopian; the first marathon to be won barefoot; the first to finish in moonlight; and the first to be run as fast as 2hrs 14mins 16.2sec.

Bikila was a member of the Palace Guard of the Emperor Haile Selassie and at 28 had run two good marathons before reaching Rome. During the gruelling 26 miles, he took no refreshment. Just before the halfway mark the Moroccan, Rhadi, took the lead and stayed there. Bikila reacted to the challenge and was more than 100 metres ahead at the finish.

Smile at the tape

From the longest to the shortest of Olympic races. And a wonderful girl from Tennessee, Wilma Rudolph. The natural successor to Australia's Betty Cuthbert, Wilma had an amazing ability to break into a wide smile as she reached the tape.

She had won a bronze in the relay in Melbourne, and now the stage was set for her to attempt the Triple Crown of sprinting. British hopes rested on the miner's daughter from Cudworth, Yorks, Dorothy Hyman. She ran splendidly but her reward was a silver in the 100m and a bronze in the 200m.

Tennessee Tigerbelles

Miss Rudolph won the 100m in a wind-assisted 11sec and the 200m in 24sec. Then she anchored the Tennessee Tigerbelles to victory in the relay in 44.5sec, a tenth of a second outside the world mark they'd set in the heats.

All that achieved by a girl born seventh in a ghetto family of 19 children. At seven years old she had contracted polio, from which she made a remarkable recovery to become known as the 'black gazelle'.

All Rome cheered for Bikila, the barefoot marathon winner, a Royal palace guard from Ethiopia, and the beautiful American, Wilma Rudolph, the black gazelle, winner of the women's 100m and 200m.

1960 Rome: Europe in the running in the sprints

For the first time in the history of the games the sprint titles went to non-English speakers. Amin Hary, a blond German built like a middleweight boxer, and a silky Italian called Livio Berruti — sun glasses and all — were the men to strike gold.

100m — won in the blocks

Hary was 23 and before arriving in Rome had been the first man to clock 10sec for the 100m. For that race Britain had Peter Radford, a genuinely fast sprinter from Wolverhampton who had set a world record of 20.5sec for the 200m. The Americans had three men in the final, Sime, Budd and Norton.

There were three false starts — two caused by Hary, but he was warned only about the second. Radford had gone well on each occasion, but when the gun went for the actual race he was left in his blocks. Hary and his false starts had upset his rivals and he raced away with the title. He won in 10.2 sec, the same time as Dave Sime, but Hary was clearly ahead.

Radford took the bronze in 10.3sec and arguably ran faster than them all to make up a disastrous deficit of four metres at the start. The race had been won by Hary in the blocks.

Chorus for Berruti

The German didn't contest the 200m and Berruti showed his ability winning all three preliminary races in 21sec, 20.8sec and 20.5sec respectively. Good sprinting, this, and he flowed round the bend into the straight for another 20.5sec time to claim a gold medal, which had had his name on it from the first of the heats. The Italian crowd went wild, chanting Berutti's name rhythmically, like the chorus of a grand opera.

Breaking the barrier

In the 400m the 45 second barrier was broken not by one man, but two. The clear favourite after the heats was the American, Otis Davis, who at 28 had only recently been selected for the American track team. He led from the halfway mark, but towards the tape the German Carl Kaufmann gobbled up the track, running right at Davis' shoulder with five metres left. The German flung himself at the tape, to be beaten by only six inches. Both men clocked 44.9sec in this unforgettable confrontation.

Otis Davis (USA) considered his 400m win was pre-determined by fate — he was wearing a vest with number 400 on it. Kaufmann of Germany was beaten by only a few inches, but insisted on taking Davis' photo.

Hary (West Germany) won the 100m in spite of three false starts, two of which he caused. Dave Sime of America took the silver and Radford (GB) the bronze. The local hero Berruti received great support from the crowd, who appreciated his style – he ran in dark glasses.

1960 Rome: Russians shock the USA in field events

The long jump title went to the amiable American, Ralph Boston, who beat the Olympic record of Jesse Owens. Earlier that summer he had beaten Owens' world mark, which had lasted since 1935. Owens was the first man to congratulate Boston.

John Thomas (USA) was clear favourite for the high jump. All he had to do was stand up to win. That was until two Russians came along. Robert Shavlakadze, who took the gold and 19 year-old Valeriy Brumel, who took the silver.

Tarzan of the pole

The pole vault, however, did go according to plan with the Californian, 'Mr Muscles', Don Bragg soaring 4m 70cm. Only men with fibre glass poles (not then used in the Olympics) have gone higher. Bragg, like Weissmuller before him, was later called to Hollywood to be yet another King of the Jungle in Tarzan films.

Parry O'Brien, winner of the shot in 1952 and 1956, settled for the silver behind a winning put of 19m 68cm by his fellow American, Bill Nieder. Al Oerter (USA), in the second of his long series of wins, retained his discus title with a throw of 59m 18cm.

British wilt

All team managers knew that there were only two ways to beat Rome's heat and humidity. Go early and acclimatise, or go at the last moment to minimise the effect. The British took an unsatisfactory middle course and their only athletics champion was walker Don Thompson, who had trained in his steam-filled bathroom in Middlesex. Every British competitor except the sprinters wilted in the heat.

Vlassov (USSR) was not only weightlifting gold medalist, he was also an army colonel at 26, a poet and he spoke four languages.

Ralph Boston beat Jesse Owens' long jump record. Owens was there to congratulate him.

Intellectual weightlifter

Not so the Soviet weightlifter, Yuri Vlassov, who at 3am on a Sunday morning lifted an amazing combined total of 537.5kg (1,184½ lbs) to obliterate the previous world record. Not for nothing was he hailed the strongest man on earth. And at the same time he must have been one of the most academically gifted of the athletes. He was a poet, a Colonel at 26, spoke four languages and often helped out as an interpreter.

Far away in the Bay of Naples the crown prince of Greece became king of the Dragon Class yachting. Later as King, Constantine was forced to abdicate when the generals took over his country.

Don Bragg went from pole vault gold to a contract to play Tarzan. Prince Constantine of Greece lived up to family Olympic traditions in sailing.

Top: A joyous moment as the American Wilma Rudolph achieves the sprint double by winning the 200m.

Bottom: The agony and the ecstasy of Herb Elliott who smashed the field and the world record in the 1,500m final of 1960 in Rome.

1960 Rome: USA and Australia divide swimming spoils

At the Stadio del Nuoto the Americans ruled the waves. Australian swimmers searched for the form they showed in Melbourne. But someone compared the American and Australian performances to champagne and flat beer. For all that the Australian flag was hoisted many times and any other nation would have been delighted with the results.

A title contested

One title, after all these years, is still the subject of debate — the men's 100m. John Devitt of Australia was given the verdict in a world record 55.2sec. But Lance Larson (USA) had apparently touched first. The electric timing and slow motion film put Larson first, but two out of three first place judges gave the Australian the verdict. Strangely, two out of three second place judges claimed Devitt as well.

Murray Rose and John Konrads had two great tussles, with Rose winning the 400m and Konrads the 1,500m. In this race the American George Breen took the bronze as he had in 1956.

The Americans took both relays, both diving titles and in all 11 golds compared to Australia's five. That spirited young lady from Sydney, Dawn Fraser, was still too good for the world in the 100m.

Breaking the duopoly

The only swimming title the Americans and Australians missed was the women's 200m breaststroke. There the Yorkshire girl, Anita Lonsbrough, triumphed in a world record time of 2mins 49.5sec, half a second ahead of the German Wiltrud Urselmann.

The Turks came to the fore in the wrestling and won seven gold medals, but overall the dominating nation in Rome was clearly the Soviet Union. They won 43 golds to America's 34. And in all medals, the Russians collected 103 against 71 by the States.

There was one bad moment in a games relatively free of controversy. Under the broiling afternoon sun in the 100km cycling road race, the Dane Knud Jensen, fell and later died in hospital. At first the cause seemed to be sun-stroke, but then ominous traces of drugs were discovered.

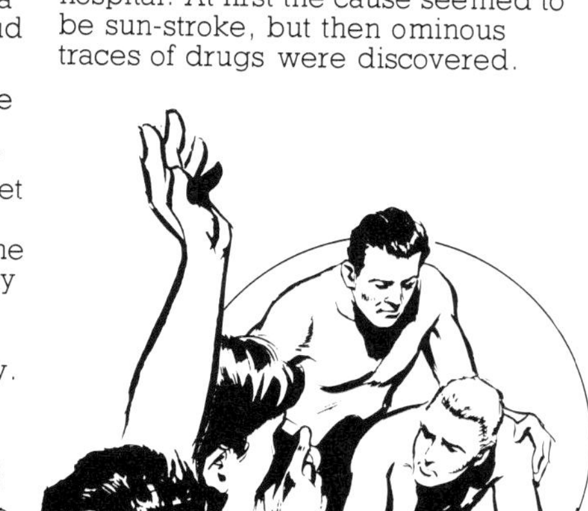

The men's 100m swimming title is still disputed. Australian John Devitt was given the gold medal, although the electronic timing put Larson first.

Rose and Konrads (Australia) met in two epic tussles. Rose took the 400m and Konrads the 1,500m.

Denmark's cyclist Knud Jensen died after the road race. Drugs were suspected, but not proved.

Records and results: 1960

Africa awakes

In Rome in 1960 the African challenge first became a real force in the games. Between 1960 and 1972 Africans won 10 gold medals, 15 silver and 16 bronze. In 1976 the African countries withdrew from the Olympics. These are some of their results:

1960 Rome
5,000m
6. Maiyoro (Kenya)
Marathon
1. Bikila (Ethiopia) 2hrs 14mins 16.2sec
2. Rhadi (Morocco)

1964 Tokyo
800m
3. Wilson Kiprugut (Kenya)
5,000m
5. Kip Keino (Kenya)
10,000m
2. Mohamed Gammoudi (Tunisia)
4. Mamo Wolde (Ethiopia)
Marathon
1. Abebe Bikila (Ethiopia) 2hrs 12mins 11.2sec

1968 Mexico City
800m
1. Wilson Kiprugut (Kenya) 1min 44.5sec
1,500m
1. Kip Keino (Kenya) 3mins 34.9sec new Olympic record
5,000m
1. Mohamed Gammoudi (Tunisia) 14mins 0.5sec
2. Kip Keino (Kenya)
3. Naftali Temu (Kenya)
10,000m
1. Naftali Temu (Kenya) 29mins 27.4sec
2. Mamo Wolde (Ethiopia)
3. Mohamed Gammoudi (Tunisia)
Marathon
1. Mamo Wolde (Ethiopia) 2hrs 20mins 26.4sec
4 x 400m relay
2. Kenya, 2mins 59.6sec
Steeplechase
1. Amos Biwott (Kenya) 8mins 51sec

1972 Munich
400m
3. Julius Sang (Kenya) 44.92sec
800m
3. Mike Boit (Kenya) 1min 46sec
1,500m
2. Kip Keino (Kenya) 3mins 36.8sec
4. Mike Boit (Kenya)
5,000m
2. Mohamed Gammoudi (Tunisia) 13mins 27.4sec
10,000m
3. Miruts Yifter (Ethiopia) 27mins 41sec
Marathon
3. Mamo Wolde (Ethiopia) 2hrs 15mins 08.4sec
4 x 400m relay
1. Kenya 2min 59.8sec
400m hurdles
1. John Akii-Bua (Uganda) 47.82sec new world record
Steeplechase
1. Kip Keino (Kenya) 8mins 23sec
2. Ben Jipcho (Kenya) 8mins 24.6sec
3. Amos Biwott (Kenya) 8mins 33.6sec

Down under runners come up

The 1960 games saw three great talents from Australia and New Zealand. They were Peter Snell, Herb Elliott and Murray Halberg. Here are their results:

800m
1. P. Snell (NZ) 1min 46.3sec new Olympic record
2. R. Moens (Belgium)
3. G. Kerr (Jamaica)
1,500m
1. H. Elliott (Australia) 3mins 35.6sec new world record
2. M. Jazy (France)
3. I. Rozsavolgy (Hungary)
5,000m
1. M. Halberg (NZ) 13mins 43.4sec
2. H. Grodotski (Germany)
3. K. Zimney (Poland)

Wilma, queen of the track

America's Wilma Rudolph was the star woman athlete at the Rome Olympics. She won three track golds. Here are her results:

100m
1. W. Rudolph (USA) 11sec
2. D. Hyman (GB) 11.3sec
3. G. Leone (Italy) 11.3sec
200m
1. W. Rudolph (USA) 24sec
2. J. Heine (Germany) 24.4sec
3. D. Hyman (GB) 24.7sec
4 x 100m relay
1. USA 44.5sec
2. Germany 44.8sec
3. Poland 45sec

Boxers turn professional

Many of the Olympic's best boxers have turned professional and subsequently taken world titles. Here is the list to date:

Boxer	Olympic gold	World Championship	
John Field (USA)	1924 Featherweight	1929 Welterweight	1932 Welterweight
Pascual Perez (Argentina)	1948 Flyweight	1954 Flyweight	
Floyd Patterson (USA)	1952 Middleweight	1956-59 Heavyweight	1960-62 Heavyweight
Nino Benvenuti (Italy)	1960 Welterweight	1967 Middleweight	1968 Middleweight
Cassius Clay (USA) (Muhammad Ali)	1960 Light Heavyweight	1964-67 Heavyweight	1974-79 Heavyweight
Joe Frazier (USA)	1964 Heavyweight	1968-73 Heavyweight	
George Foreman (USA)	1968 Heavyweight	1973-74 Heavyweight	
Leon Spinks (USA)	1976 Light Heavyweight	1976 Heavyweight	

Top left: Steve Clark of America (left) and Britain's Bobby MacGregor, in doleful mood after losing to the great Don Schollander in the 1964 100m final.

Centre left: Don Schollander (USA) winning the 400m freestyle, on his way to collecting four gold medals in Tokyo,

Centre right: The happiness of Ann Packer (GB) as she beats the finest 800m runners in the world in 1964.

Bottom left: Peter Snell (NZ) leads the pack home in the 800m to defend the title he had won at Rome. He also won the 1,500m.

1964 Tokyo: The first of the super games

The Japanese had waited a long time to stage the Olympics. The 1940 games were planned for Tokyo, to celebrate 2,600 years of the Japanese Imperial Dynasty. But in that fateful year the world was otherwise occupied.

When their turn finally came in 1964, the Japanese set an almost suicidally high standard of preparation. Other cities since then have felt severe financial strains keeping up with the Tokyo trend. New highways, super efficiency and one of the most beautiful rowing courses ever built awaited five and a half thousand competitors. Overcrowding was becoming a problem for Olympic organisers.

The 62nd session of the IOC had unanimously re-elected Avery Brundage of America as President, but the games did not escape political debate. South Africa was banned for apartheid, Indonesia and North Korea were excluded for political interference in sport.

If some new political wounds were opened, there was an attempt to heal one from the past. Yoshinori Sakai, born in Hiroshima the day the atom bomb fell, carried the Olympic flame into the stadium.

1964 Tokyo: The flair of the first Asian games

For the first time the games moved to Asia. The Japanese, anxious to make a prestigious mark in the world, and perhaps to atone for World War II, put on the finest Olympics yet seen. With imaginative flair, the torch was lit by Yoshinori Sakai, who was born in Hiroshima one hour before the atomic bomb exploded in 1945.

Africa challenges

Seventeen African nations took part in the games. As Plato wrote, there's 'always something new from Africa'. If Rome saw the birth of African involvement in the games, Tokyo saw Africa's development into an unexpectedly strong source of competition, even if not many medals fell to Africans.

Snell's ambition

Once again the New Zealander, Peter Snell, was there. He was to be the giant of the Tokyo games. The man who surprisingly had won the 800m in Rome now toyed with opponents before actually setting foot to track.

Snell was entered for both the 800m and 1,500m. As world record-holder for the mile most thought he would concentrate on the 1,500m. The NZ press corps were convinced he would use the 800m only as a speed trial for the longer distance. But while opposition and press waited, Snell told the correspondent of the London *Evening News*: 'Only two men in Olympic history have defended their 800m title. I aim to be the third.' Then as an afterthought he said, 'And nobody has also added the 1,500m to two golds at 800m.' So it was out. Snell wanted both titles.

The opposition flounders

He won both 800m heats. That left only the Kenyan, Wilson Kiprugut. bold enough to challenge for the gold. He led the field through the bell in 52sec. But along the back-straight Snell kicked and the sea of opposition floundered on the beach of disbelief. The black vest disappeared round the 200m bend. He won unchallenged in 1min 45.1sec. Canadian Bill Crothers snatched second place from the gallant Kiprugut.

After that performance, nobody was going to take on Snell in the 1,500m. Everyone ran for the silver medal. So Snell made history with three middle distance golds in two games, by winning the 1,500m in 3mins 38.1sec, one and a half seconds ahead of the next man, Joszef Odlozil of Czechoslovakia.

The Tokyo Olympic flame was ignited by Yoshinori Sakai, born in Hiroshima the day the A-bomb fell. The Africans made their presence felt in the colourful opening ceremony and on the track. The king of the middle distance events was New Zealander Peter Snell, who took gold at 800m and 1,500m.

Left: David Hemery (GB) 400m hurdles gold, 1968.

Right: Peter Snell (NZ) 800m gold, 1960, 800m and 1,500m gold, 1964.

1964 Tokyo: Ron Clarke learns the hard way

The boy who lit the Olympic flame in Melbourne was called Ron Clarke, always the bridesmaid, never the bride on the track. Clarke had broken world records galore from 3,000m upwards. When he went to Tokyo the Australians believed this superman was capable of winning three golds. But running against the clock is different from running against men. And poor Ron was destined to find out the hard way.

A Sioux rides in

On a cold wet night at the end of the first day's events 38 runners went out for the 10,000m. Clarke held the world record and led the field most of the way. But try as he might he couldn't open up a gap. On the final lap an American named Billy Mills was twice impeded by lapped runners, but he surged up the final 100m to defeat both the fancied Gammoudi of Tunisia and Clarke. Mills had run the race as a warm up for the marathon from which he promptly withdrew! He was half Sioux Indian and a US marine.

First US double

Clarke hoped for better things in the 5,000m. But still hung-over from the earlier defeat, he was no match for the rest and finished ninth. Bob Schul (USA) was the surprise victor in 13mins 48.8sec. It's the only time Americans have achieved the distance double. Harald Norporth of Germany was second and another American, Bill Dellinger, third.

That left the marathon as Clarke's last remaining target. But again he finished ninth. The winner was the magnificent Abebe Bikila, who dominated the race throughout. Only one man challenged him, Jim Hogan of Ireland. He hung on gamely for 20km but by then he was broken. Bikila finished almost four minutes ahead of the English silver medalist, Basil Heatley. Hogan learned from the experience, though, and two years later in British colours, he won the European marathon title in Budapest.

Australian Ron Clarke hoped for three golds. He was beaten in the 5,000m by Schul and in the 10,000m by Mills, both Americans.

Clarke's last hope was the marathon. But he had to reckon with Bikila of Ethiopia, barefoot winner in 1960. This time he wore shoes, dominating the race throughout.

1964 Tokyo: Two world records and four UK golds

The long jump competitions provided Britain with an amazing double. Amazing because few people outside the UK had heard of Lynn Davies, a good-looking Welshman from Nantymoel in Glamorgan.

Lynn the leap

The day was wet and windy — just like Cardiff Arms Park! Lynn the Leap transfixed his opponents with a fifth jump of 8m 7cm. This put the pressure on the world recordbreakers, Ralph Boston (USA) and Igor Ter Ovanesyan (USSR). Neither liked jumping with a head wind and, although Boston did reach 8m 3cm with his final fling, it was not enough. Davies had won Britain's first field event gold since 1908.

This one for my baby

Then came the double. Mary Rand told reporters before her contest 'I'm doing this one for my baby Allison', her three year-old daughter left at home in Henley. She set a new world record of 6m 76cm to beat the favourite, Tatyana Shchelkanova (USSR) into third place. Second was a 19 year-old Pole, Irena Kirszenstein, who, as Mrs Szewinska, was later to become a great force in women's athletics. Mary Rand went on to complete the set by taking a silver in the pentathlon and a bronze in the relay.

There were both tears of sorrow and tears of joy for another English girl, Ann Packer. She was favourite for the 400m, but a gust of wind on the home stretch upset her rhythm. The Australian, Betty Cuthbert, the heroine of Melbourne, ran through it to win in 52sec with Miss Packer second.

Have a go!

Robbie Brightwell, later to marry Miss Packer, persuaded her to have a go at the 800m. She finished fifth in her heat and third in her semi-final. But in the final Miss Packer, who had been a long jumper, sprinter, and quarter-miler, put everything together and romped home in a world record 1min 01.1sec. The French girl, Dupereur, led the field round the final bend, when Miss Packer's sprinting experience took her home like an arrow.

The British athletics team left Tokyo with four golds, five silvers and three bronze medals. Only the USA and USSR did better in track and field competitions.

Britain's long jump stars both scored gold. Lynn Davies found the wet and windy conditions suited him. Mary Rand set a new world record. Ann Packer came second in the 400m, her event, but won gold and a world record in the 800m.

1964 Tokyo: Three American giants

In a land of small people three American giants captivated the hearts of the spectators with truly magnificent athletic displays. Each in his own way wrote a new chapter in Olympic history, and none more so than discus thrower, Al Oerter. Twice before he had won the title and now the world record-holder Danek of Czechoslovakia, was in the ring to halt his sequence of gold medals.

Oerter's third gold

With four throws gone, Oerter was trailing Danek and his US team-mates Weill and Sylvester. But champions are made of stern fibre, and with his fifth throw Oerter hurled out 61m. The gold medal was his.

Speed from leg power

Then there was the magical sprinting of Bob Hayes, standing 1m 82cm (6ft) tall and weighing 86kg (189.5lb). He proved that weight is no enemy to speed, with a wind assisted 9.9sec in the heats. No man had ever run that fast before. But then no one ran quite like Hayes. All movement from the waist up he kept to a minimum. All his energy was directed into leg power In the final he clocked 10sec and had two metres in hand over the second man, Enrique Figuerola (Cuba) Harry Jerome (Canada) was third, clocking 10.2sec. Later Hayes ran the last leg of the 4 x 100m relay in which the USA won in a world record 39sec.

Dallas Long, still only 23, had already been among the medals in Rome. And before Tokyo he had improved the world shot mark to 20m 66cm. He was one of the so-called invincibles who lived up to his reputation.

Long the longest

Long knew his team-mates Matson and O'Brien would push him hard. But he hadn't expected a serious challenge from the Hungarian, Varju. O'Brien, seeking a fourth gold, threw 19m 20cm, but both Long and Matson soon put the shot beyond the 20m mark. Long finally reached 20m 33cm — 13cm clear — to be hailed as one of the all-time greats of the shot put circle. Matson took the silver and Varju pipped the great O'Brien for the bronze.

Discus thrower Al Oerter (USA) made history by winning his event for the third time.

Bob Hayes won the 100m gold and later became a football professional.

Dallas Long won the shot, although challenged by Hungary's Varju.

1964 Tokyo: US dominates; Australia shows the flag

Swimmers from the United States dominated the pool. They produced 34 finalists out of a possible 39. They won eight golds, eight silvers and eight bronze medals. Don Schollander won four titles.

Happiness is golden

What a swimmer and what an Olympian! Schollander, fair-haired and good-looking, came from Oregon and was studying at Yale University. With an effortless style he won the 100m freestyle from Britain's Bobby McGregor in 54sec; he won the 400m freestyle in 4min 12.2sec, way ahead of the German, Weigand; and then he anchored the USA teams in the 4 x 100m and 4 x 200m sprint relay squads. He might have won two more golds had he not passed up the opportunity to swim in the medley relay and the 1,500m.

The Australians, recognised as the main challengers to American swimming supremacy, found themselves outclassed by a young, happy and talented band who seemed to be simply enjoying the Olympic experience. The happy team atmosphere was translated into wonderful performances that made them the most popular single squad in Tokyo.

You Tarzan, me Dawn

But while the Australians experienced disappointment there were moments of high drama for them. There was a wonderful swim by Dawn Fraser who made history by winning her speciality, the 100m freestyle, for the third successive time. With 20m to go a young Californian, Sharon Stouder, came up to the shoulder of the champion.

Dawn glanced sideways, saw the danger and sprinted home in 59.9sec, faster than the great Johnny Weissmuller. Dawn is the only swimmer to win the same title three times.

The Emperor's flag

Dawn was famous for her high spirits and tomboy antics. One night she souvenired the Japanese flag from the Emperor's Palace. When the police chased her she dived into the moat and swam away in record time! When she was finally caught, the Emperor made her a gift of the flag!

Another Australian, Kevin Berry, the double Commonwealth champion, was too hot for the Americans in the 200m butterfly. He shattered them with a world record 2min 6.6sec in the final.

American swimmer Don Schollander's effortless style won him four gold medals, including two relays.

Kevin Berry, one of the four Australians to challenge US swimmers, took a world record in the 200m butterfly.

Tomboy antics by Australia's Dawn Fraser. She souvenired the Japanese Emperor's flag.

Records and results: 1964

Dawn of a champion

Tomboy Australian swimmer Dawn Fraser is still the only swimmer to win the same event in three consecutive Olympics — Melbourne, Rome, Tokyo.

Women's 100m freestyle

1956

1. Dawn Fraser (Australia) 62 sec
2. Lorraine Crapp (Australia) 62.3sec
3. Faith Leech (Australia) 65.1sec

1960

1. Dawn Fraser (Australia) 62.1sec
2. Chris von Saltza (USA) 62.8sec
3. Natalie Steward (GB) 63.1sec

1964

1. Dawn Fraser (Australia) 59.5sec
2. Sharon Stouder (USA) 59.9sec
3. Kathy Ellis (USA) 1min 0.8sec

Dawn's other results

1956

1. 4 x 100m relay
2. 400m freestyle

1960

2. 4 x 100m medley relay
2. 4 x 100m freestyle relay
5. 400m freestyle

1964

2. 4 x 100m freestyle relay
4. 400m freestyle

Schollander's run of gold

In Tokyo the American swimmer of the games was Don Schollander. He took four golds, winning two for relays. Here are his results:

100m freestyle

1. Don Schollander (USA) 53.4sec
2. Bobby McGregor (GB) 53.5sec
3. Hans-Joachim Klein (W. Germany) 54 sec

400m freestyle

1. Don Schollander (USA) 4min 12.2 sec new world record
2. Frank Wiegand (Germany) 4min 14.9sec
3. Allan Wood (Australia) 4min 15.1sec

4 x 100m freestyle relay

1. USA (Clark, Austin, Ilman, Schollander) 3min 32.2sec new world record
2. Germany 3min 37.2sec
3. Australia 3min 39.1sec

4 x 200m freestyle relay

1. USA (Clark, Saari, Ilman, Schollander) 7min 52.1sec new world record
2. Germany 7min 59.3sec
3. Japan 8min 03.8sec

Everlasting Oerter

Al Oerter, the American discus champion has set new Olympic records and taken the gold at four games. He is in training for Moscow.

1956

1. A. Oerter (USA) 56.36m (184ft 10½ins) new Olympic record
2. F. Gordien (USA)
3. D. Koch (USA)

1960

1. A. Oerter (USA) 59.18m (194ft 1½ins) new Olympic record

1964

1. A. Oerter (USA) 61m (200ft 1½ins) new Olympic record

1968

1. A. Oerter (USA) 64.78m (212ft 6ins) new Olympic record
2. G. Milde (Germany)
3. L. Daneck (Czech.)

Medved — three golds, three weights

Russian freestyle wrestler Alexandr Medved at his best weighed 105kgs (231lbs) yet he was able to defeat giants like Taylor (USA) who weighed 190.5kg (419lbs or almost 30 stones)! In three games Medved won at three different weights:

1964

Light heavyweight (bodyweight limit 97kg)

1. A. Medved (USSR)
2. A. Ayik (Turkey)
3. S. Mustafar (Bulgaria)

1968

Heavyweight (bodyweight over 97kg)

1. A. Medved (USSR)
2. O. Duralyer (Bulgaria)
3. W. Dietrich (W. Germany)

1972

Super heavyweight (bodyweight over 100kg)

1. A. Medved (USSR)
2. O. Duralyer (Bulgaria)
3. C. Taylor (USA)

Cycling medals 1896-1964

Until 1964 Italy was much the most successful Olympic cycling nation, with a total of 16 gold medals, against nine by her nearest rival, France. Since 1964 Italy has lost her domination of cycling events, although she is still among the medalists.

Date	Individual road race	1,000m sprint	1,000m time trial	4,000m team pursuit
1896	A. Konstantinidis (Greece)	—	—	—
1912	R. Lewis (South Africa)	—	—	—
1920	H. Stenqvist (Sweden)	M. Peeters (Holland)	—	Italy
1924	A. Balchonnet (France)	L. Michard (France)	—	Italy
1928	H. Hansen (Denmark)	R. Beaufrand (France)	W. Falck-Hansen (Denmark)	Italy
1932	A. Pavesi (Italy)	J. van Egmond (Holland)	E. Gray (Australia)	Italy
1936	R. Charpentier (France)	T. Merkens (Germany)	A. van Vliet (Holland)	France
1948	J. Beyaert (France)	M. Ghella (Italy)	J. Dupont (France)	France
1952	A. Noyelle (Belgium)	E. Saachi (Italy)	R. Mockridge (Australia)	Italy
1956	E. Baldini (Italy)	M. Rousseau (France)	L. Faggin (Italy)	Italy
1960	V. Kapitonov (USSR)	S. Gaiardoni (Italy)	S. Gaiardoni (Italy)	Italy
1964	M. Zanin (Italy)	G. Petenella (Italy)	P. Sercu (Belgium)	W. Germany

Top right: Bob Beamon's amazing long jump in Mexico. His world record of 8.90m (29ft 2½ins) still stands.

Top left: King and queen of the swimming pool in 1972, Mark Spitz (USA) and Shane Gould (Australia), with a total of ten gold medals between them.

Bottom left: Rodney Pattisson and Christopher Davies (GB) winners of the 1972 Flying Dutchman class yachting.

SPIETH

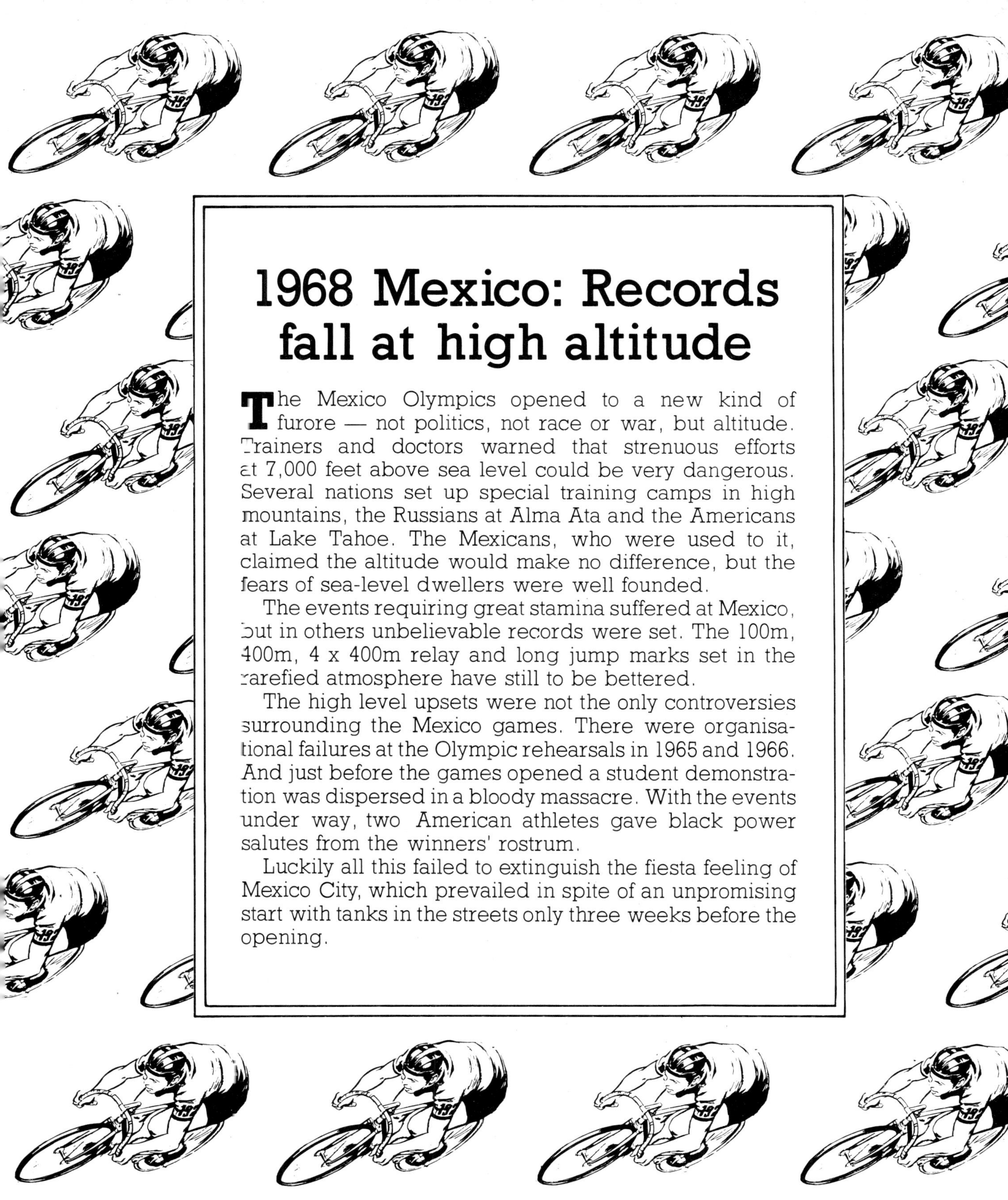

1968 Mexico: Records fall at high altitude

The Mexico Olympics opened to a new kind of furore — not politics, not race or war, but altitude. Trainers and doctors warned that strenuous efforts at 7,000 feet above sea level could be very dangerous. Several nations set up special training camps in high mountains, the Russians at Alma Ata and the Americans at Lake Tahoe. The Mexicans, who were used to it, claimed the altitude would make no difference, but the fears of sea-level dwellers were well founded.

The events requiring great stamina suffered at Mexico, but in others unbelievable records were set. The 100m, 400m, 4 x 400m relay and long jump marks set in the rarefied atmosphere have still to be bettered.

The high level upsets were not the only controversies surrounding the Mexico games. There were organisational failures at the Olympic rehearsals in 1965 and 1966. And just before the games opened a student demonstration was dispersed in a bloody massacre. With the events under way, two American athletes gave black power salutes from the winners' rostrum.

Luckily all this failed to extinguish the fiesta feeling of Mexico City, which prevailed in spite of an unpromising start with tanks in the streets only three weeks before the opening.

1968 Mexico: Politics and race, controversy at altitude

The state of Mexico has a violent history. On top of the famous pyramids Aztec priests tore out the hearts of men as sacrifices to their gods. The Spanish conquistadores under Cortes fought bitter wars to conquer the country. The Inquisition sacrificed more souls to another god.

On the eve of the games of the XIX Olympiad violence erupted again. This time in the Square of the Three Cultures where students and trade unionists held a demonstration. Bullets ripped into the crowd from a helicopter and then soldiers moved in from all sides.

Disputed death toll

The Government put the death toll at 34. Others placed it as high as 400. Whatever the total there was no disguising the fact that the military had fired on citizens. A dark shadow fell across the Olympic Village and competitors were loth to travel into town.

Controversy surrounded the very decision to hold the games in Mexico, at an altitude of 7,200ft. Leading coaches and sportsmen proclaimed that Olympic exertion at such height might cause deaths.

Black power

Then came the Black Power controversy when the American negro, John Carlos, raised a clenched fist to the crowd at the victory ceremony in which he gained a bronze. He and two other Black Power militants were sent home.

The third controversy involved the medical problems of exertion at altitude: Mexico is 7,200 feet above sea level. Some athletes needed oxygen, others set records impossible at sea level.

One Sunday morning in the athletes village fighting broke out between Polish competitors and competitors from French-speaking West African countries. The Africans were playing music on the lawn outside the Polish quarters. The Poles bombarded their rivals with water bombs, which led to fist fights, complaining that they had been kept up all night by 'jungle music'.

Once again the ideal of Olympic comradeship had fallen by the wayside.

Three controversies raged over the Mexico games: firstly, student demonstrations were put down in a bloody political confrontation; secondly, two American athletes gave the Black Power Salute on the winner's podium.

1968 Mexico: Africans at home in the distance events

In spite of the inauspicious opening, the Mexican people made sure that there was a friendly atmosphere in the city. For the first time a woman lit the flame at the opening ceremony. And as soon as the games began it was obvious that the African mountaineers would take over the gruelling distance events, showing the advantage of those who lived at rarefied heights.

The Kisii Hill kings

But even allowing for altitude, the Kenyans from the Kisii Hills were wonderful athletes. Two years earlier they had dominated the same events at the Commonwealth Games in the steamy, lowland heat of Jamaica.

Kip Keino, already a much respected competitor, had dropped out of the 10,000m and was beaten into second place in the 5,000m. But in the 1,500m there was no doubting his mastery, even though the world record-holder, Jim Ryun (USA) turned in a top class run. Try as he might Ryun couldn't hold the Kenyan on the final lap and Keino won in 3min 34.9sec, an Olympic record.

Mohamed Gammoudi (Tunisia) just pipped Keino and another Kenyan, Naftali Temu, in the 5,000m.

Temu, the Commonwealth six mile champion, had his own back in the 10,000m which he won by 0.6sec in 29min 27.4sec. Mamo Wolde of Ethiopia was second and Gammoudi third.

The other Ethiopian

Then came Wolde's chance of Olympic greatness. Abebe Bikila pulled out of the marathon because of injury, telling everyone that his Ethiopian colleague would win. And win Wolde did, in style. He raced through the heat and thin atmosphere in 2hrs 20mins 26.4sec, more than three minutes ahead of the next man.

Kenya won a third track gold with Amos Biwott in the steeplechase.

For the first time a woman carried the Olympic flame into the stadium.

The Africans were wonderful athletes who made full use of their altitude experience in the distance events. Keino took the 1,500m ahead of Ryun (USA). Mamo Wolde (Ethiopia) won the marathon after his team mate Bikila dropped out.

1968 Mexico: American sprinters all the way

The Mexico Games broke all records for the number of people and nations taking part — 7,490 competitors represented 112 countries — 18 more than the previous best at Tokyo. In all, 252 Olympic records were broken and Africa passed another milestone of progress on the track.

Winners are American

As usual, it was American competitors who dominated the sprints. For the first time the 10sec barrier was beaten in the 100m, and the 20sec barrier in the 200m. Over the longer distance Tommie Smith and John Carlos embarked on a private duel. They were both products of San Jose University, California, and both were strong advocates of a movement called the Olympic Project for Human Rights. Smith won the final, flowing round the track in 19.8sec and, surprisingly, the Australian Peter Norman snatched the silver from Carlos.

Then came the unfortunate demonstration by Carlos, as a result of which he was sent home. Smith told reporters that the Carlos incident was understandable. 'When we're winning we're Americans. Otherwise we're Negroes,' he said.

Jim Hines, a beautifully balanced runner, won the 100m in 9.9sec and then helped the US relay squad to a gold medal.

Americans in relays

The 400m was totally dominated by US athletes; clearly Tommie Smith's world record of 44.5sec would be under pressure. Lee Evans clocked 44.8sec in his semi-final with Larry James one tenth slower. In the final Evans gave an immaculate display of power running. He needed it because James dogged his footsteps all the way. But Evans held his rhythm, didn't tie up, and got the verdict by a metre in a world record 43.8sec.

The third American qualifier, Freeman, took the bronze. Then this trio teamed up with Matthews to win the 4 x 400m relay in another world mark of 2min 56.1sec with Kenya second and West Germany third.

Wyomia Tyus (USA) won the women's 100m and anchored the relay team to success. But the 200m title went to the Polish girl, Irena Szewinska in 22.5sec, another world record.

After the 100m semi-final Greene (USA) needed treatment because of altitude. Hines (USA) won.

Another world record in the 200m. Smith (USA) threw his arms in the air as he crossed the line.

1968 Mexico: Jumping at new heights

'We came to Mexico expecting someone to jump 28 feet. But we still haven't seen it.' These words were spoken by a dejected Lynn Davies who had come to defend his long jump title, and had seen his dreams smashed by the very first leap of Bob Beamon.

One was enough for Beamon

People in America were saying that one day Beamon would put together his sprint run-up, his high trajectory and powerful kick. And on the afternoon of Friday, 18 October, Beamon went into orbit, stunning two world record-holders and the reigning champion with a leap of 29ft 2½ins (8m 90cm). It was Beamon's one and only jump in Mexico! Not only has no one matched that since, but with the 1980 games approaching no one has even reached 28 feet!

Lynn Davies glanced at Ralph Boston and said: 'I can't go on. What's the point?' Boston didn't answer, neither did the Russian Igor Ter Ovanesyan. Davies went on to beat Beamon several times at sea-level, but up there in the thin air nobody could challenge him. It's a matter of record that the second man, Klaus Beer of East Germany was 71cm (2ft 4ins) behind the winner.

The women too

The women's long jump was won in exactly the same fashion by the Rumanian girl, Victoria Viscopeanu. The Sheffield girl, Sheila Sherwood, was favourite and opened with a personal best 6m 60cm. A few minutes later Viscopeanu powered along the runway, soared into the air and smashed the world record with a distance of 6m 82cm (22ft 4½ins). This was enough to give her victory, with Mrs Sherwood second and the Russian Tatyana Talysheva taking the bronze.

The Canadian girl, Debbie Brill, winner of the 1979 World Cup high jump, developed a method of jumping backwards. It was called the Brill Roll. Then the 6ft 4in American, Dick Fosbury, copied the technique, which was renamed the Fosbury Flop and became the high jumping sensation of Mexico. It brought Fosbury the title with a jump of 2m 24cm (7ft 4½ins), although the world record eluded him.

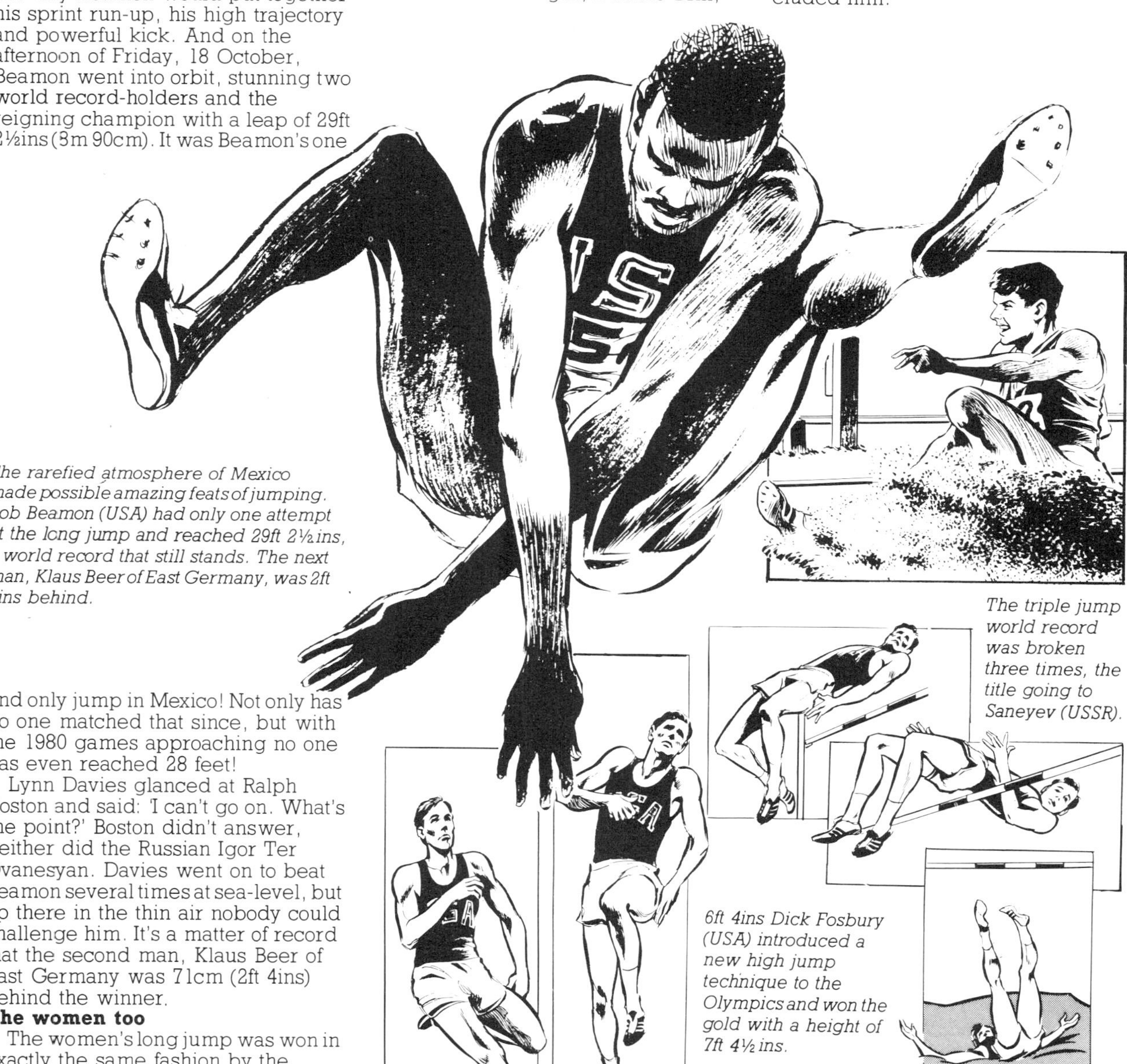

The rarefied atmosphere of Mexico made possible amazing feats of jumping. Bob Beamon (USA) had only one attempt at the long jump and reached 29ft 2½ins, a world record that still stands. The next man, Klaus Beer of East Germany, was 2ft 4ins behind.

The triple jump world record was broken three times, the title going to Saneyev (USSR).

6ft 4ins Dick Fosbury (USA) introduced a new high jump technique to the Olympics and won the gold with a height of 7ft 4½ ins.

1968 Mexico: British gold, but not for Lill

Lillian Board, a young blonde from Ealing, was Britain's Golden Girl. She was attractive, with a sunny disposition, and she ran fast times from 100 to 440yds. She was favourite for the 400m title and ran like the favourite in the heats. In the final she ran faster than ever before, but she had to settle for the silver.

Besson's perfect timing

When the Yugoslav, Vera Nikolic, pulled out of the competition Miss Board appeared to have little to worry about. But the Olympic finals are fraught with danger. The London girl blazed into the lead. She was ahead at the 200m mark in 24.5sec, and surged round the final bend into the home straight. But closing in was the French sprinter, Collette Besson, who timed her dash to perfection. She took the lead at the one point where a challenge is unanswerable — 5m from the tape. She won in 52sec with Miss Board a tenth of a second behind. Tragically Miss Board never had another chance to compete in the Olympics. She died of cancer on Boxing Day 1970, at the age of 22.

Hemery's calculations

Britain was to have a victory on the track and it came from the Boston-educated David Hemery who gave as perfect a display of 400m hurdling as the world will ever see. He won in a world record 48.1sec with the second man, Hennige of West Germany, 10 metres behind. John Sherwood, husband of Sheila, romped home in third spot. 'I had worked it out mathematically,' Hemery said afterwards. 'And it all went according to my figures.'

The discus also went according to plan, when the ever popular Al Oerter came, saw and conquered the world of discus throwing in his fourth successive games. With his third attempt he moved slowly, almost lethargically, in the circle and then unleashed a whiplash throw. The discus flew 64m 78cm, an Olympic record and a personal best. Oerter now had four golds — one for each of his children.

Lillian Board narrowly missed gold in the 400m, and never had a second chance. She died of cancer two years later.

David Hemery of Britain set a new world record in the 400m hurdles, having planned the race mathematically.

Al Oerter's fourth gold – one for each of his children. He will be back in the discus contest in Moscow.

1968 Mexico: Caslavska, everyone's gymnast darling

'Music provides the gymnastics of the soul, and gymnastics are the music of the body.' Yehudi Menuhin. Perhaps nobody exemplified this description more than the beautiful Czech girl, Vera Caslavska.

In the Mexico Auditorio, normally the centre for concerts and ballet, Vera made Olympic history by adding four gold medals to the three she had won at Tokyo. In the one event she did not win, she took the silver medal.

Vera Caslavska, the Czech gymnast, swept the board with four gold medals. The crowds went wild when she performed floor exercises to the Mexican Hat Dance. While in Mexico she married her team-mate, Odlozil.

With the Russian invasion of Czechoslovakia still uppermost in people's thoughts, Miss Caslavska had everybody on her side. When she chose the 'Mexican Hat Dance' as her music for the floor exercises she brought the house down. Never was an Olympic competitor more loved by an audience.

Vera had spoken out against the Russian invasion and at one stage blacked her face and hair with coal dust to escape the clutches of the invader. But she arrived in Mexico fully prepared for the task ahead, and gave so perfect and charming a performance that still she ranks with the greatest — even allowing for the later exploits of Olympic heroines such as Nadia Comaneci, Nelli Kim and Olga Korbut. Heart throbs all, and Caslavska was the first. During her stay in Mexico she capped her performance with a colourful wedding to her 1,500m team-mate, Joszef Odlozil.

Horses in water courses

Up in the heights of Avandaro, torrential rains made the three day riding event a marathon of awesome proportions. Small streams became torrents, firm ground turned to mud. But the British, under the leadership of a former tank commander, 54 year-old Derek Allhusen, won the team golds with Allhusen taking the individual silver.

At the Stadio Olimpico, Marian Coakes, on *Stroller* and David Broome on *Mr Softee* took silver and bronze medals in the Grand Prix Show Jumping.

Rain made the three day event hazardous. Britain won medals in show jumping.

1968 Mexico: Two against American might

Like an avalanche the Americans descended on the Olympic Pool and swept out their opponents. 23 gold medals, 15 silver, 20 bronze — more than all the rest put together.

Little Miss Debbie Meyer, aged 16 from Sacramento, had the toughest schedule of all. Yet she won the 200m, the 400m and the 800m to give an all-round display of freestyle swimming that made a mockery of both altitude and her rivals. Her times were 2min 10.5sec, 4mins 31.8sec and 9min 24sec. All well outside her records for the distances, but all well ahead of her competitors.

Don Schollander, the star of Tokyo, picked up a silver in the 200m and a gold in the 4 x 200m relay. A young man named Mark Spitz was also a member of the squad. More of him later.

But two men did stand out and temporarily halt the American march on the medal table . . . Roland Matthes of East Germany and the Australian sprinter, Mike Wenden. In the 100m, the blue riband event of swimming, Wenden, an 18 year-old from Liverpool, New South Wales, took on the might of America and beat the lot. He clocked 52.2sec to outsprint both Ken Walsh and Spitz. In the 200m the Australian turned for home with Schollander and John Nelson on his tail. But again his powerful stroke took him to gold.

East German example

The deceptively strong Matthes controlled his tempo in both the back-stroke events. In the 200m he was lying fifth with 55m to go. But on each occasion he steamed past his American rivals. In both the 100m and 200m back-stroke events American swimmers came second, third and fourth. But ahead of them was the man who, unknown at the time, was blazing a trail which East German swimmers were to follow.

Debbie Meyer won three freestyle golds for America.

Matthes showed what East German swimmers could do.

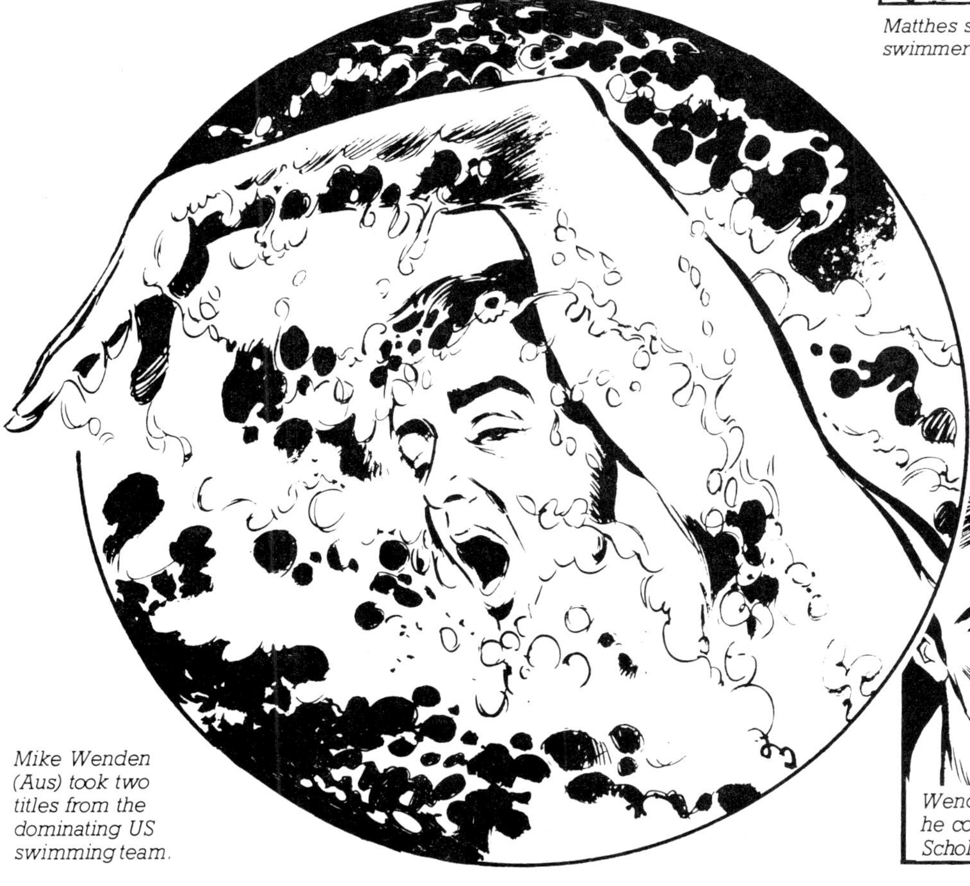

Mike Wenden (Aus) took two titles from the dominating US swimming team.

Wenden's trainer convinced him he could beat stars like Schollander and Spitz.

Records and results: 1968

Comparing the great gymnasts

Five women — Latynina, Caslavska, Tourischeva, Korbut and Comaneci — are without doubt the greatest women gymnasts seen at the Olympic games. How would they compare if they all competed with each other, when they were all at their best? We shall never know, but we can add up their points to date and see!

No. of gold medals each	Individual	Team	Total
Larissa Latynina (USSR) 1956, 1960, 1964	6	2	8
Vera Caslavska (Czechoslovakia) 1964, 1968	7	-	7
Ludmilla Tourischeva (USSR) 1968, 1972, 1976	1	3	4
Olga Korbut (USSR) 1972, 1976	2	2	4
Nadia Comaneci (Rumania) 1976	3	-	3

No. of points each	Latynina	Caslavska	Tourischeva	Korbut	Comaneci
Combined exercises (average mark)	19.258	19.562	19.656	19.506	19.818
Vault	19.283	19.775	19.650	19.175	19.625
Asymmetric bars	19.416	19.650	19.425	19.450	20.000
Beam	19.382	19.575	19.475	19.725	19.950
Floor exercises	19.599	19.675	19.825	19.575	19.750
Overall average	19.387	19.647	19.606	19.486	19.828

Beamon's bounce

The 1968 men's long jump was decided with Bob Beamon's first jump. The American cleared 8.90m (29ft 2½ins), setting a new world record, 45cm better than ever before, and 78cm more than the previous Olympic record.

The world's leading long jumpers

Bob Beamon (USA)	8.90m	29ft 2½ins
Larry Myricks (USA)	8.52m	27ft 11½ins
Nenad Stekic (Yugoslavia)	8.45m	27ft 8¾ins
Ralph Boston (USA)	8.35m	27ft 4¾ins
Igor Ter-Ovanesyan (USSR)	8.35m	27ft 4¾ins
Jozef Schwarz (West Germany)	8.35m	27ft 4¾ins
Arnie Robinson (USA)	8.35m	27ft 4¾ins

Flying in Acapulco Bay

In the Flying Dutchman class sailing two Britons demolished all opposition. In sailing your placings count as points, so the fewer points the better! These are the results achieved by Rodney Pattisson and Ian MacDonald-Smith:

Race No.	1	2	3	4	5	6	7	Points Total
1. Britain	1*	1	1	1	1	1	2	3
2. W. Germany	1	3	2	2	13	21	7	43.7
3. Brazil	14	7	4	3	3	10	1	48.4

* *Finished first, later disqualified.*

No wonder they won, their boat was called 'Supercalafragelisticexpialidocious'!

Triple jump, triple winner

Soviet triple jumper Victor Saneyev has won this event for the last three Olympic games. Here are his results:

1968 Mexico City
1. V. Saneyev (USSR) 17.39m (57ft 9½in) new Olympic record
2. N. Prudencio (Brazil)
3. G. Gentile (Italy)

1972 Munich
1. V. Saneyev (USSR) 17.35m (56ft 11in)
2. J. Drehmel (E. Germany)
3. N. Prudencio (Brazil)

1976 Montreal
1. V. Saneyev (USSR) 17.29m (56ft 8¾in)
2. J. Butts (USA)
3. F. Wartenburg (E. Germany)

The sprint double

The ambition of the greatest sprinters has been to take both 100m and 200m events. Seven men have written their name into Olympic history.

Date	100m	Country	Time	200m	Country	Time
1904	Archie Hahn	USA	11 sec	A. Hahn	USA	21.6sec
1912	Ralph Craig	USA	10.8sec	R. Craig	USA	21.7sec
1928	Percy Williams	Canada	10.8sec	P. Williams	Canada	21.8sec
1932	Eddie Tolan	USA	10.3sec	J. Owens	USA	21.2sec
1936	Jesse Owens	USA	10.3sec	E. Tolan	USA	20.7sec
1956	B-J Morrow	USA	10.5sec	B-J Morrow	USA	20.6sec
1972	Valery Borzov	USSR	10.14sec	V. Borzov	USSR	20 sec

The medals to date

Until the 1960s the Americans' predominance in the medal scores was unchallenged. Since then countries like Russia and East Germany have eroded the US lead.

Country	gold	silver	bronze	total
USA	545	397	354	1296
USSR	161	155	150	466
Britain	141	173	147	461
Germany (E. and W.)	122	169	153	444
France	116	133	124	373
Sweden	116	110	136	362
Italy	105	92	87	284
Hungary	96	77	89	262
Finland	80	69	93	242
Australia	55	45	59	159

Top left: In the rarified air of Mexico, Britain's David Hemery is crowned the grand master of hurdling, with a world record over 400m.

Centre left: Chris Finnegan handing out some punishment to the American Alfie Jones in their middle-weight semi-final in Mexico. Finnegan went on to win the gold medal.

Centre right: The American sprint relay team giving the Black Power salute after winning their event in 1968.

Bottom right: Champions both, Johnny Weissmuller and Don Schollander, two of the greatest swimmers from the US.

Above: Biwott (Kenya), Malinowski (Poland) and Villain (France) lead the 1972 steeplechase final.

Right: Renate Stecher (E. Germany) 100m and 200m gold, 1972.

1972 Munich: Violence clouds golden games

The 1972 games were a fine demonstration of technical brilliance. But even the rich West Germans blanched slightly at the bill — over £300 million. All appointments were lavish, and the stadium was a masterpiece of innovation in poles, cables and translucent plastic. For added convenience all facilities, except the sailing, were located in an area of one square mile.

Unfortunately anything which attracts the worldwide attention of the Olympic games, tends to suffer from unwanted political attention as well. In Munich there were the wonderful sporting achievements of Spitz, with seven gold medals, double golds by Viren and Borzov, and legendary performances by Shane Gould, Korbut and Kato. But what everyone remembers is the violence of the Palestinian raid on the Israeli team headquarters.

With seven athletes dead, the games continued in a mood of mourning and sadness. A memorial service was held for those who were killed. A senseless blow had all but extinguished the Olympic spirit. Many visitors left Munich before the games were over.

1972 Munich: Spitz wins all superlatives

The games in Munich opened with some spectacular swimming. During the first week 30 world records and 84 Olympic marks were bettered or equalled. Never had the Olympics seen such sparkling performances in the pool. And never had one man dominated the games the way Mark Spitz did.

Record list of golds

The American superman won seven golds, two more than the record set by the gymnast Anton Heida in 1904. Spitz went through his Olympic apprenticeship at Mexico and was now unbeatable. Immediately after the games the young man from Modesta, California, turned his Olympic exploits into spot cash, bringing in a reputed 5 million dollars. During the games Spitz caused trouble with the IOC by waving a pair of famous training shoes at the crowd. This was deemed advertising but he was exonerated by the committee of investigation.

Failed in Mexico

Four of his golds came in the sprints. The man who in Mexico had proclaimed his ability to win four individual golds, and failed to win any, was now ice-cool and super trained. Built like a boxer, he was a man of iron in every respect.

Spitz smashed the world record in the 100m with a sizzling time of 51.22 sec, and then did likewise in the 200m with 1min 52.78sec. With him in the relay teams there was never any doubt that the Americans would take both titles in style. Spitz, the last man to swim, helped the USA to more world records with 3min 26.42sec in the 4 x 100m, and 7mins 35.78sec in the 4 x 200m.

Then he switched to the butterfly. He had broken world marks in the American trials, so it was inevitable that he would do the same in Munich. He won the 100m 'fly in 54.27sec and the 200m in 2 mins 7 sec. Just for good measure, he swam the butterfly leg in the 4 x 100m medley relay and again struck gold in world record time.

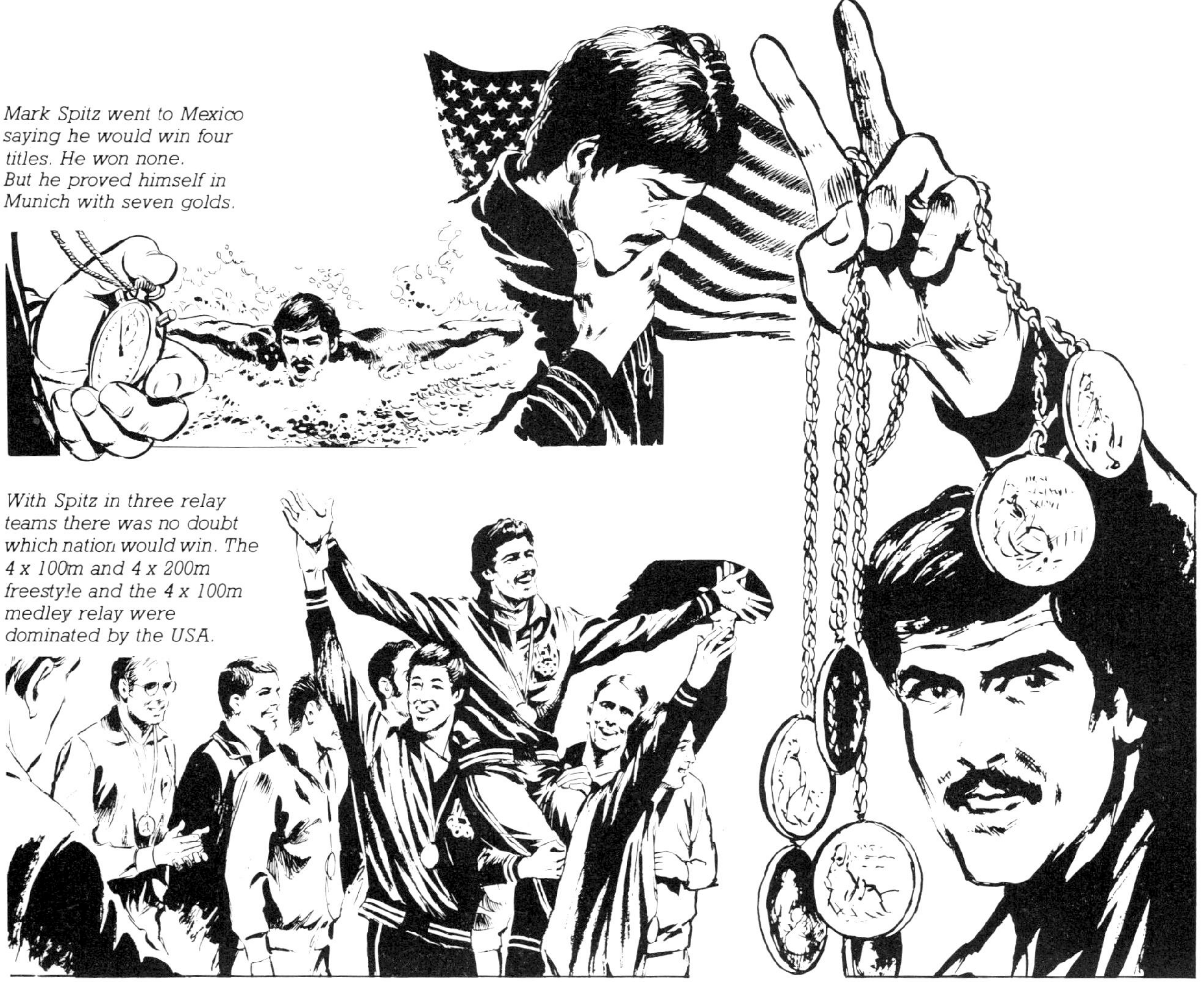

Mark Spitz went to Mexico saying he would win four titles. He won none. But he proved himself in Munich with seven golds.

With Spitz in three relay teams there was no doubt which nation would win. The 4 x 100m and 4 x 200m freestyle and the 4 x 100m medley relay were dominated by the USA.

1972 Munich: Shane's koala brings her luck

Shane Gould, a pretty blonde from Australia, was only 15 but aware of both her good looks and her winning potential. Before leaving for the games she insisted that her dentist remove the brace on her teeth so she could look her best. Everywhere at the swimming stadium she clutched her koala bear, and the mascot proved lucky. Miss Gould won three golds, a silver and a bronze — a feat not achieved by any other woman swimmer before her.

Queen of the Schwimmhalle

She smashed the world record for the 200m, the 400m and the 200m record and the world record in the 200m.

And in the women's back-stroke a 15 year-old Virginian, Melissa Belote, did the double in fine style. She led from start to finish in both races beating the Hungarian Andrea Gyarmati in the 100m and Sally Atwood (USA) in a world record 2mins 19.19sec in the 200m.

The Americans dominated the swimming with 29 golds. The Australians won six. Sweden and Japan won two each, as did East Germany — a hint of what was to come in Montreal.

Also only 15, Melissa Belote (USA) won the 100m backstroke gold, then the 200m backstroke with a world record as well.

At 15, Shane Gould of Australia won three golds, a silver and a bronze in Munich. Her toy koala bear mascot was with her all the time. On the victory podium someone handed her another mascot, a kangaroo.

individual medley, that supreme test of all-round ability comprising the freestyle, back-stroke, breast-stroke and butterfly. Before the 800m final Miss Gould was asked how she felt. 'Every race is hard. I'm tired, but I shall do my best.' Her best brought her a silver medal behind Kathy Rothhammer of the USA who set new world figures.

Miss Gould was queen of the Schwimmhalle, where Spitz was king. But for sheer sportsmanship none bettered the American Tim McKee who twice plunged into the water to hug the man who had beaten him in the 200m and 400m individual medley events, Gunnar Larsson of Sweden. Here was the true spirit of the Olympics.

A hint of things to come

From East Germany, Roland Matthes, the back-stroke star of Mexico, paddled through the water like a steamer to break the 100m Olympic

Roland Matthes, having starred in Mexico, took the men's backstroke double – 100m and 200m – showing the way for East German swimmers who were to make such an impression in Montreal.

1972 Munich: Viren, the latest of the Flying Finns

In 1970, the man who had coached New Zealanders Peter Snell and Murray Halberg to Olympic golds went to Finland. Once again Arthur Lydiard succeeded. This time with the Flying Finns Pekka Vasala and Laase Viren.

Viren, a policeman from beyond the Arctic Circle, demonstrated to the world the Finn's love of running by dominating the 5,000m and 10,000m events — more so than even Zatopek.

Britain's hopes dashed

In the 10,000m Britain had high hopes in Dave Bedford who had been breaking records for two seasons. Belgium expected Emil Puttemans to bring them glory, and Ethiopia put its faith in Miruts Yifter.

Viren destroyed Bedford halfway through the race, in almost the same way that Kuts had brought Pirie to his knees in 1956. And when Puttemans set out on a prolonged challenge over the last two laps he found that the blue-and-white vested Finn came from the same mould as Nurmi. Viren resisted all attacks and came down the home straight like a miler to win in the world record time of 27mins 38.4sec.

In the 5,000m, Viren coasted through to the final without showing any pace. In the final a tactical battle ensued with nobody willing to open up the race, until the American Steve Prefontaine darted away with four laps to go. Viren responded immediately taking with him the title holder, Mohamed Gammoudi of Tunisia. Viren outstayed his rivals, kicked again at 200m from the tape and strode home in a world record 13mins 26.4sec.

Vasala scored again for Finland in the 1,500m, taking the title in 3min 36.3sec, with the holder, Kip Keino, second and another Lydiard man, Rod Dixon (NZ), in third spot.

Dave Bedford (GB) was disappointing in the 10,000m

Gammoudi (Tunisia) and Viren (Finland) fell, but Viren still won the 5,000m in world record time.

Vasala won another gold for Finland in the 1,500m, beating the title holder Kip Keino (Kenya) and Rod Dixon (NZ).

1972 Munich: Borzov, Soviet sprinting by numbers

The Soviet Union has produced only one world class sprinter and he had been discovered in a most bizarre way. Years before the Munich games Russian experts fed statistics into a computer — body weight, height, muscle power, leg stride and shape, all formulated as a mathematical equation. The answer that came out was Valery Borzov who at Munich proved the equation to have been correct.

One man show

He won the 100m in 10.14sec, the 200m in 20sec and anchored the Russians to a silver in the sprint relay. With a one man show Borzov took Russian sprinting to the top of the world, but he remains a solitary success story in this sphere. The Soviet masterminds have yet to reproduce their successful experiment.

Borzov won three heats and the final of the 100m beating Taylor (USA) and Miller (Jamaica) into the minor placings. His European record held until September 1979, when Pietro Mennea broke it in Mexico.

Then came the 200m; again nobody finished ahead of the square-framed Russian. He surged round the bend in the final straight with a power-packed display of sprinting. He struck the tape with more than a metre in hand over the American, Black. The Italian, Mennea, gained the bronze.

Renate, the German Express

The women's sprints were similarly dominated by an East German, Renate Stecher. This girl became more and more difficult to beat as the games wore on. She was the first European to achieve the sprint double since Fanny Blankers-Koen in 1948.

There was none of the supple smoothness of Wilma Rudoph in this girl's style — eyes ahead, total concentration, power running over the final 50 metres.

Raelene Boyle of Australia had a magnificent start in the 100m and with 30m gone she was ahead. But then along came the German Express, with an unanswerable pickup that destroyed all opposition. She clocked 11.07sec with Miss Boyle on 11.23sec.

The 200m was just as dramatic. Stecher was matched stride for stride by Boyle until the halfway mark. But the jet finishing Renate strode away up the home stretch for a decisive victory in 22.40sec — a metre ahead. Poland's Irena Szewinska — second to Mary Rand in the 1964 long jump — took the bronze.

Protesters sent home

The Americans Mathews and Collett finished first and second in the 400m final. But they were sent home in disgrace after giving the Black Power salute as the Stars and Stripes were raised at the victory ceremony.

Valery Borzov is the solitary Soviet success story of sprinting. His 100m and 200m victories justified the Russians' scientific search for a sprint king.

Mathews and Collett (USA) were sent home after their victory podium demonstration.

1972 Munich: An Irish smile wins hearts and a gold

Heide Rosendahl, the darling of the home crowd, sprinted down the runway to clear 6m 78cm with her first leap in the long jump. The girl, who had tasted the bitterness of injury in Mexico and lost her chance of pentathlon gold, leaped almost as high again at the announcement of her distance, and then had to sweat it out while Diana Yorgova of Bulgaria and Eva Suranova of Czechoslovakia inched nearer and nearer the magic mark.

Home crowd with her

With one round to go the Bulgarian girl was one centimetre behind the leader. And as she was jumping last of all, the tantalising competition kept the audience captive and rooted to their seats. Yorgova put everything into a do or die effort. She roared down the runway and soared into the air. But the red flag went up. She had fouled the take-off marker. In an anti-climax ending to a wonderful competition, Rosendahl was the triumphant heroine while Yorgova hung her head in dejection at winning *only* a silver medal!

'It's the loneliest place in the world,' she said afterwards. 'Everyone remembers the champion, nobody recalls who came second.'

Mary's shot wins a record

When she was 21 and living in Lancashire, Mary Peters told her father she wanted bags of cement as a birthday present! Her wish was fulfilled and her dad made a shot put circle for her. For ten years she represented Britain in the shot. And it was this event which gave her the gold medal against the challenge of Rosendahl not in the shot, but in the pentathlon.

Mary, by 1972 working back in her native Belfast, scored 960 points for her shot putting while Miss Rosendahl could muster only 830. This lead of 130pts proved absolutely decisive, as Mary won the title by a mere ten points with a world record total of 2801pts.

Local girls beaten

The girl from Northern Ireland beat into third place Burglinde Pollack (GDR). But such was the happy disposition and ebullient character of the Irish girl that she managed to endear herself to the partisan German crowd, even though two of their girls had to settle for silver and bronze. Mary's Irish eyes have always been smiling, and this attitude helped her to strike gold.

Peters was a popular winner, even though she beat West Germany's Rosendahl.

Mary Peters' shot put gave her a world record pentathlon score.

Heide Rosendahl pleased local crowds with a long jump gold and pentathlon silver.

1972 Munich: No such thing as a certainty

With the Olympics you can be sure of only one thing: there's no such thing as a certainty. At Munich two of the most unexpected victors — in the 800m and the marathon — appeared as if by magic.

Hats off to Wottle

Dave Wottle, wearing a battered golf hat, had entered the US trials only as a test of his speed for the 1,500m. Yet he won these trials equalling the world record time. As a youth he had suffered fractures in both legs, he sustained an achilles tendon injury before the games and he arrived in Munich on honeymoon. Never was a man apparently less prepared for Olympic stardom.

Yet Wottle, not the most elegant of runners, possessed total belief in the one thing he could do better than anyone else in 1972, hammer out the final 50 metres of a race like a sprinter.

Stumbling for the silver

After running second in his heat, Wottle beat the highly ranked German, Franz-Jozef Kemper in the semi-finals. Kemper and his East German rival, Dieter Fromm, were certainly better runners, while the Russian Evgeni Arzanhov, was arguably the best man in the final.

In the event the Russian stumbled two strides from the tape and this cost him a gold medal. The American powered through to win by three hundredths of a second in 1min 45.9sec — the same time as Arzanhov — with Mike Boit of Kenya one tenth of a second further behind.

Dave Wottle (USA) wearing a golf hat, ran from the back to break through and win the 800m. He was on honeymoon in Munich!

Wottle defeated three fancied runners in the 800m, Fromm (East Germany), Boit (Kenya) and Arzanhov (USSR).

The Shorter marathon

Frank Shorter, a fine distance runner, was not at that time very well known outside the USA.

Shorter was born in Munich and he ran through the streets as though they belonged to him. The British runner, Ron Hill, and the Australian Derek Clayton, were the strong men for the first 10km. But then Shorter put in an amazing burst of speed over the following five kilometres to burn off his rivals. He maintained his pace to the 20km station and then coasted home in 2hrs 12mins 19.8sec.

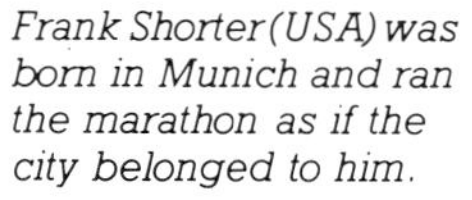

Frank Shorter (USA) was born in Munich and ran the marathon as if the city belonged to him.

1972 Munich: British and US favourites fail

David Hemery, Olympic 400m hurdles champion in Mexico, had won the Commonwealth high hurdles titles in 1966 and 1970. So he arrived in Munich solid favourite to retain his title. His world record of 47.1sec still stood and he looked good winning his heat.

Confidence shattered

A Ugandan named John Akii-Bua was quite fast in his heat, but in the semi-finals he found himself in a commanding position having destroyed the confidence of both Hemery and the powerful American, together in the same race and Akii-Bua beat them both in 49.25sec. Ralph Mann. They were all drawn

Then there was that hurdler extraordinary, Rod Milburn (USA). His expert start and powerful style took him through the 110m event unbeaten. He scorched home in the final in 13.24sec — just outside the world record — and way ahead of the Frenchman Guy Drut.

By the day of the hurdles finals Akii-Bua and Milburn were both favourites. But in the javelin and pole vault the top men came unstuck.

Pole vaulter Bob Seagren held the world record at 5m 63cm and as the Americans had always won the pole vault he seemed the natural choice.

But from East Germany came the European champion, Nordwig.

He was a well seasoned campaigner, who had suffered only rare defeats. He failed twice to clear lesser heights at his first attempt, but at 5m 45cm he went over first time and Seagren buckled. Nordwig improved to 5m 50cm to emphasise his superiority.

There was another shock in store in the javelin. Klaus Wolfermann of West Germany reached 88m 40cm with his fourth throw to unseat the champion and world record-holder, Janis Lusis of the Soviet Union.

Lusis (USSR) was the javelin favourite and Seagren (USA) the pole-vault favourite. Both lost unexpectedly.

Akii-Bua of Uganda who defeated two favourite hurdlers, Hemery (GB) and Mann (USA) in the 400m

Milburn (USA) the bearded, head-banded favourite, made no mistake in the hurdles.

Mann took the second spot and Hemery was third.

In that order they finished the final. Akii-Bua smashed the world record with a time of 47.82sec leaving the rest of the field to contest the minor placings. Mann took second place by a hundredth of a second.

1972 Munich: Olga captures the hearts of millions

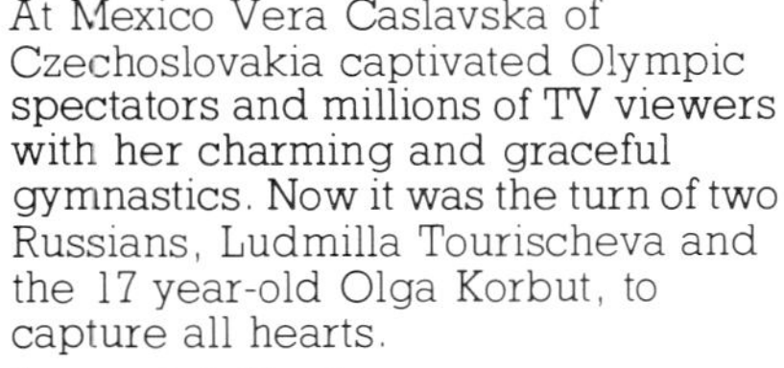

At Mexico Vera Caslavska of Czechoslovakia captivated Olympic spectators and millions of TV viewers with her charming and graceful gymnastics. Now it was the turn of two Russians, Ludmilla Tourischeva and the 17 year-old Olga Korbut, to capture all hearts.

Immortal display

Tourischeva was unquestionably the female star of the games, but it was little Miss Korbut who became the superstar of the small screen. Tourischeva won that most testing of all gymnastic competitions, the combined exercises, in which Miss Korbut finished way down in seventh position.

There was something of the Shirley Temple in Korbut. She had only to flutter her eyelids to have the spectators leaping from their seats. Rarely has a Russian brought such warmth to the games and received such spontaneous applause.

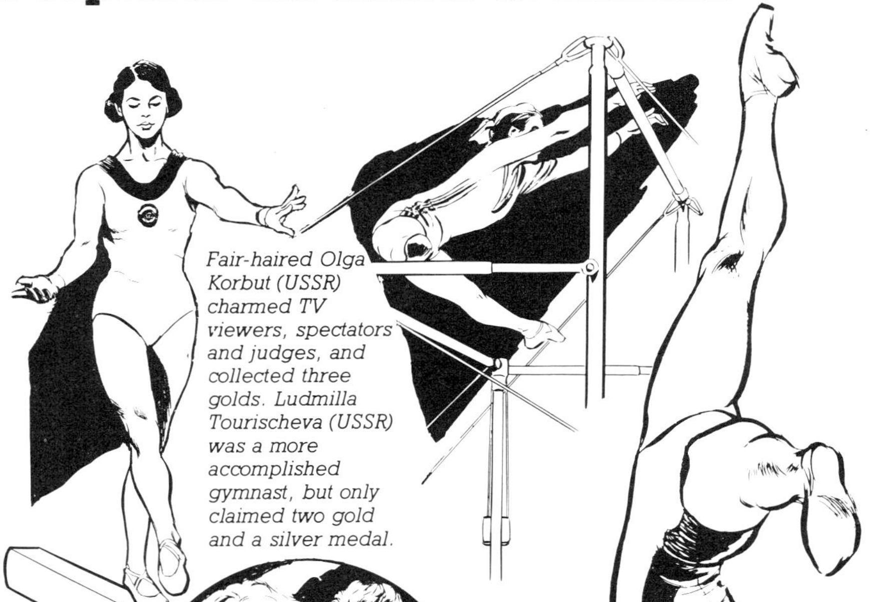

Arguments raged for days after the competitions. Was Olga really better than Tamara Lazakovitch in the beam? Was she really .025pts better than Tourischeva in the floor exercises?

The fans thought so, the judges voted so. Three golds went round the girlish neck of Olga Korbut. Tourischeva took two and a silver. The Russian girls were virtually unbeatable, but the East Germans did manage to snatch two golds through Karin Janz's performance at the vault and asymetric bars. They finished second to the Russians in the team event.

Graceful Japanese men

The Japanese dominated the men's team event. In the combined exercises it was Kato first, Kenmotsu second and Nakayama third. They brought grace and dignity to the games which saw one of the highest standards of men's gymnastics. Kato also won the parallel bars with Nakayama winning the rings.

Fair-haired Olga Korbut (USSR) charmed TV viewers, spectators and judges, and collected three golds. Ludmilla Tourischeva (USSR) was a more accomplished gymnast, but only claimed two gold and a silver medal.

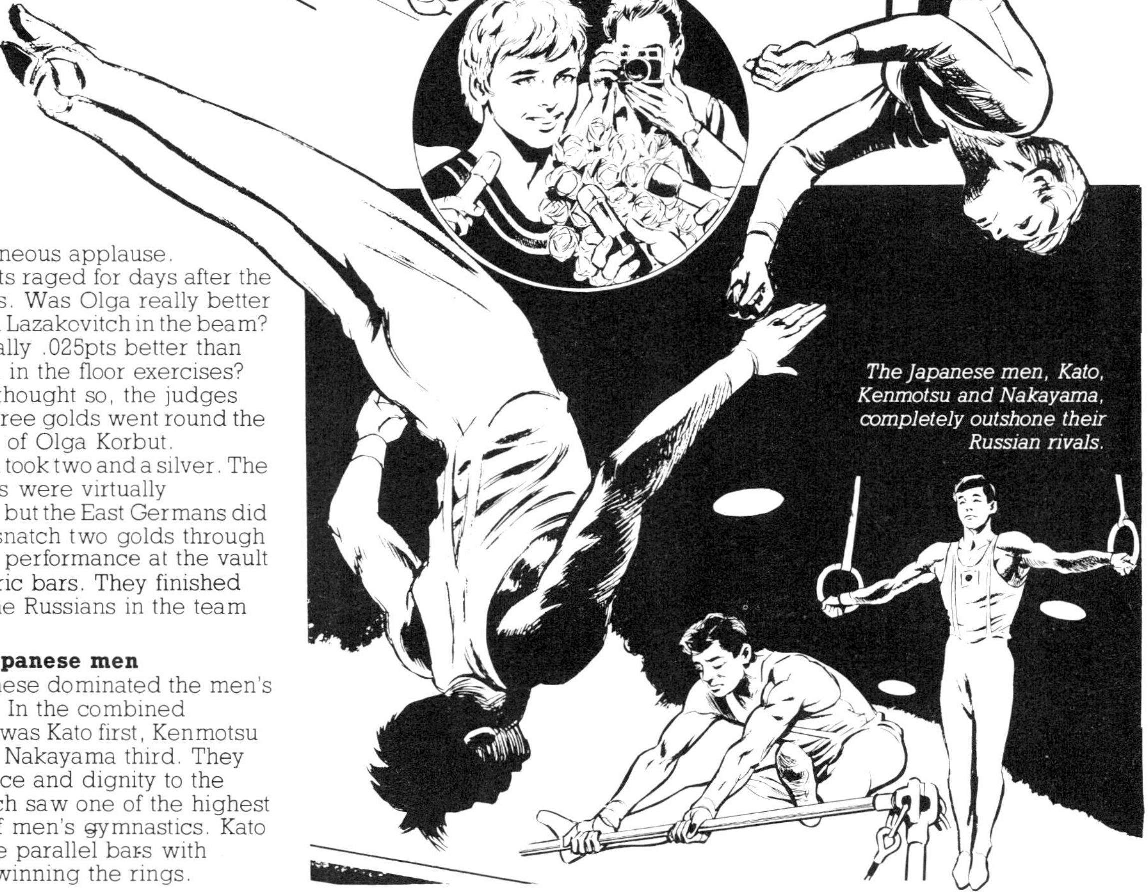

The Japanese men, Kato, Kenmotsu and Nakayama, completely outshone their Russian rivals.

1972 Munich: The heavies of the he-man events

The leviathan of the games was the American Chris Taylor, who weighed in at 190.5 kilos — 30 stones — for the super-heavyweight freestyle wrestling competition. But size was not enough for the man who made the scales wince. He met, and fell to, a man almost half his size, Alexandr Medved of Russia.

Speed beats weight

Medved, a man nimble on his feet, was to wrestling what the dancing Gentleman Jim Corbett had been to prize fighting. Medved used all his speed and ringcraft to tie the American fortress into knots. And the Russian ended with a gold in three successive Olympics, a record in the sport.

Weight lifts weight

Another man of giant proportions was Vasily Alexeev. He was expected to have strong competition from Rudi Mang (West Germany), Ken Petera (USA) and Serge Reding (Belgium).

The canny Russian knew too much for his rivals. In the press-and-snatch events he lifted well within his range, but his rivals over-strained to build up leads. Then in the jerk, Alexeev rounded off an excellent performance with a combined total of 640kg, an Olympic record.

Weight behind the shot

Twice before the he-man of Polish athletics, shot-putter Wladyslaw Komar, had been to the games, and twice before he had lost. This time a formidable array of American talent stood in his way, but with a very first heave of 21m 18cm, the giant Pole put on the pressure.

With a sort-that-one-out smile at his rivals, he sat down to wait out the next five rounds. Nobody could match his distance and the American, George Woods, had to be content with another silver to go with the one he took at Mexico.

With Al Oerter out of the discus reckoning after four golden Olympics, the title went to Europe when big Ludwig Danek of Czechoslovakia, at last, had his chance. He had won silver in 1964 and bronze in 1968. His determination finally paid off.

Polish shot putter, Wladyslaw Komar had been to two previous Olympics. This time he overcame heavy US opposition to win a gold.

Two giant Russians – Alexeev, the weightlifter, who won the super heavyweight and set a new Olympic record; and Medved who beat 30-stone American Taylor to win a freestyle wrestling medal for the third Olympics running.

1972 Munich: Doubtful sportsmanship in basketball

After winning 63 consecutive Olympic matches, and having won all six basketball competitions in previous games, it was the clock that finally beat the Americans in Munich. They had been up against it throughout the final, and at one stage they were as far as ten points behind the Russians.

With three seconds remaining the US team took the lead for the first time. Doug Collins put away two penalty shots giving them a 50-49 lead as the buzzer went. The Basketball Federation ruled a further three seconds must be played because of an earlier timing mistake. The Russians sent a long ball to their 2m player Alexandr Bielov who promptly netted, to give a score of 51-50. Again the buzzer went.

Americans walk out

The Russians had won. The crowd erupted. The Americans left the stadium refusing to accept their silver medals. Their Olympic President, Cliff Buck, said he would recommend the USA to pull out of future Olympic basketball competitions. This threat was never carried out.

Big hit boxer

The big hit of the boxing was, of course, Teofilo Stevenson, the heavyweight from Cuba. He followed in the footsteps of George Foreman and Joe Frazier as the heavyweight champion. Cassius Clay had won the light heavyweight title in Rome and all three went on to win the world title in the ranks of the very-well-paid professionals.

Fighting for Fidel

'Not for me,' said Stevenson, 'I'm fighting for Fidel Castro and I'll be back at Montreal.' Stevenson was a sensation. He won his first fight in the opening round. Then he stopped Duane Bobick (now a leading contender for the world crown) in round three. Stevenson overcame his semi-final opponent, Peter Hussing of West Germany in the second round. He didn't even have to fight in the final because his opponent, Ion Alexe of Rumania, climbed into the ring with an alleged thumb fracture.

Stevenson was rightly voted the fighter of the games. But determined efforts by American promoters to draw him into professional boxing failed. He did, however, offer to meet Muhammad Ali over three rounds in Havana.

In the basketball final unexpected extra time gave an extra point and victory to USSR for the first time ever.

The American team protested and refused to accept its silver medals.

U.S.S.R. 51

U.S.A. 50

Heavyweight boxing favourite, Teofilo Stevenson of Cuba, easily defeated his opponents for a well-earned gold. He later refused offers to turn professional like his predecessors Clay, Frazier and Foreman.

25KG

1972 Munich: The shadow of political violence

The deeds of September the 5th, 1972, rank with the most infamous of modern times. The Palestinians chose that date to invade the Israeli quarters in the Olympic village. Two Israelis were killed almost immediately. The Palestinians took hostages and eventually the German police agreed to the terms laid down by the Palestinians.

The invaders left with their hostages for a nearby airfield where a helicopter was waiting. Also waiting were the West German Police. The Black September group walked straight into the ambush. A further fifteen lost their lives. It has never been proved which bullets caused the deaths, Palestinian or Police. But 11 Israelis died that day, one athlete, two weight-lifters and two wrestlers, four coaches and two judges. The last six had asked to go as hostages, in order to prevent competitors from being endangered.

The show goes on

The dead and the remainder of the Israeli team were flown home. A day of mourning was called. Avery Brundage, President of the IOC, announced that the games would go on.

The atmosphere at the Olympic Stadium was funereal. Most competitors and all journalists wanted to leave immediately.

But the IOC held the view that the games must go on to show would-be imitators of the Black September group that they were not open to blackmail.

The great escape

It was a debatable argument and few in the athletes' village agreed. But the show went on, and finished a day late on Sunday, September the 10th. The popular answer to the IOC decision was seen at Munich airport, where a great escape was taking place. People were fighting to get the first flights out of a city in which suddenly an atmosphere of festivity had turned into the melancholy of a morgue.

The Palestinian Black September guerrilla group was responsible for the death of 11 Israelis after a kidnapping and shoot-out. Avery Brundage of the IOC decreed that the games go on. Athletes mourned.

Records and results: 1972

Spitz — the magnificent seven

In Munich Mark Spitz (USA) won seven golds.

100m freestyle
1. Mark Spitz (USA) 51.22sec, new world record
2. Jerry Heidenreich (USA) 51.65sec
3. Vladimir Bure (USSR) 51.77sec

200m freestyle
1. Mark Spitz (USA) 1min 52.78sec, new world record
2. Steve Genter (USA) 1min 53.73sec
3. Werner Lampe (West Germany) 1min 53.99sec

100m butterfly
1. Mark Spitz (USA) 54.27sec, new world record
2. Bruce Robertson (Canada) 55.56sec
3. Jerry Heidenreich (USA) 55.74sec

200m butterfly
1. Mark Spitz (USA) 2mins 00.70sec new world record
2. Gary Hall (USA) 2mins 02.86sec
3. Robin Backhaus (USA) 2mins 03.23sec

---

4 x 100m freestyle relay
1. USA (Edgar, Murphy, Heidenreich, Spitz) 3mins 26.42sec new world record
2. USSR 3mins 29.72sec
3. East Germany 3mins 32.42sec

---

4 x 200m freestyle relay
1. USA (Kinsella, Taylor, Genter, Spitz) 7mins 35.78sec new world record
2. West Germany 7mins 41.69sec
3. USSR 7mins 45.76sec

---

4 x 100m medley relay
1. USA (Stamm, Bruce, Spitz, Heidenreich) 3mins 48.16sec new world record
2. East Germany 3mins 52.12sec
3. Canada 3mins 52.26sec

Gould's glorious golds

Shane Gould almost matched Spitz's performance in the pool.

100m freestyle
1. Sandra Neilson (USA) 58.59sec new Olympic record
2. Shirley Babashoff (USA) 59.02sec
3. Shane Gould (Australia) 59.06sec

200m freestyle
1. Shane Gould (Australia) 2mins 03.56 sec new world record
2. Shirley Babashoff (USA) 2mins 04.33sec
3. Keena Rothhammer (USA) 2mins 04.92sec

400m freestyle
1. Shane Gould (Australia) 4mins 19.04sec new world record
2. Novella Calligaris (Italy) 4mins 22.44sec
3. Gudrun Wegner (East Germany) 4mins 23.11sec

800m freestyle
1. Keena Rothhammer (USA) 8mins 53.68sec new world record
2. Shane Gould (Australia) 8mins 56.39sec
3. Novella Calligaris (Italy) 8mins 57.46sec

200m individual medley
1. Shane Gould (Australia) 2mins 23.07sec new world record
2. Kornelia Ender (East Germany) 2mins 23.59sec
3. Lyn Vidali (USA) 2mins 24.06sec

Heavyweight lifts super weight

Vasily Alexeev of Russia established new Olympic records in all lifts and his total in 1972. In 1976 he set a new world record as well.

1972
1. V. Alexeev (USSR)
   press 235kg new Olympic record
   snatch 175kg new Olympic record
   jerk 230kg new Olympic record
   total 640kg (1410¾lb) new Olympic record
2. R. Mang (West Germany) total 612kg
3. G. Bonk (East Germany) total 572kg

1976
1. V. Alexeev (USSR)
   snatch 185kg new Olympic record
   jerk 255kg new Olympic record
   total 440kg (969¾lb) new Olympic record
2. G. Bonk (East Germany) total 405kg
3. H. Losch (East Germany) total 387.5kg

American monopoly broken

From 1896 to 1968 the USA won the pole vault at every Olympics. But in 1972 the US domination was broken.

1896
William Hoyt (USA) 3.30m (10ft 9¾ins)
1900
Irving Baxter (USA) 3.30m (10ft 9¾ins)
1904
Charles Dvorak (USA) 3.50m (11ft 6ins)
1908
Edward Cooke (USA) 3.70m (12ft 2ins)
1912
Harry Babcock (USA) 3.95m (12ft 11½ins)
1920
Frank Foss (USA) 4.09m (13ft 5ins)
1924
Lee Barnes (USA) 3.95m (12ft 11½ins)
1928
Sabin Carr (USA) 4.20m (13ft 9¼ins)
1932
William Miller (USA) 4.31m (14ft 1¾ins)
1936
Earle Meadows (USA) 4.35m (14ft 3¼ins)
1948
O. Guinn Smith (USA) 4.30m (14ft 1¼ins)
1952
Robert Richards (USA) 4.55m (14ft 11ins)
1956
Robert Richards (USA) 4.56m (14ft 11½ins)
1960
Don Bragg (USA) 4.70m (15ft 5ins)
1964
Fred Hansen (USA) 5.10m (16ft 8¾ins)
1968
Bob Seagren (USA) 5.40m (17ft 8½ins)
1972
Wolfgang Nordwig (GDR) 5.50m (18ft 5¼ins)

Above: Wilkie (GB) 200m breaststroke gold, 1976.

Below: Ender (E. Germany) 4 gold, 1976.

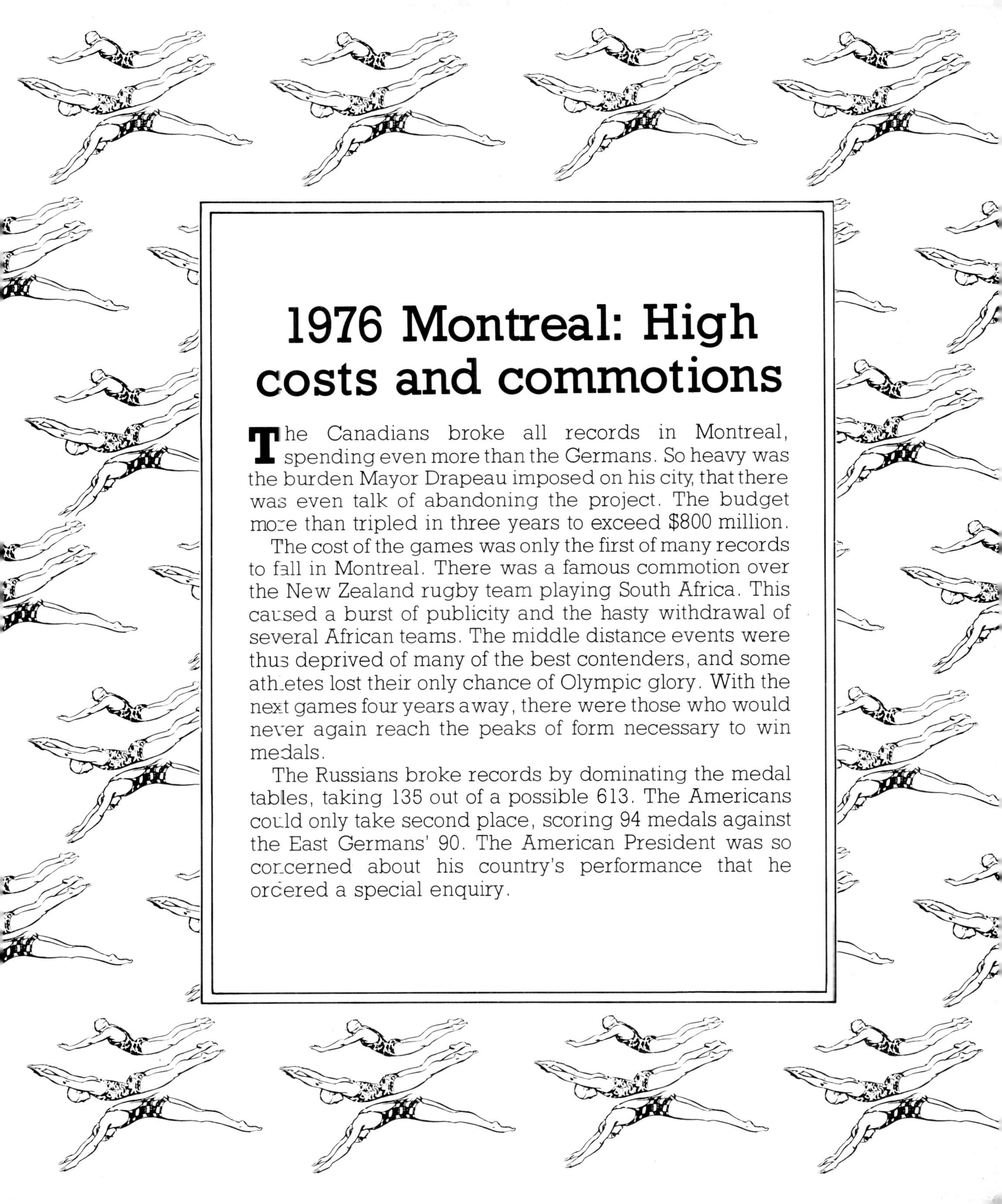

1976 Montreal: High costs and commotions

The Canadians broke all records in Montreal, spending even more than the Germans. So heavy was the burden Mayor Drapeau imposed on his city, that there was even talk of abandoning the project. The budget more than tripled in three years to exceed $800 million.

The cost of the games was only the first of many records to fall in Montreal. There was a famous commotion over the New Zealand rugby team playing South Africa. This caused a burst of publicity and the hasty withdrawal of several African teams. The middle distance events were thus deprived of many of the best contenders, and some athletes lost their only chance of Olympic glory. With the next games four years away, there were those who would never again reach the peaks of form necessary to win medals.

The Russians broke records by dominating the medal tables, taking 135 out of a possible 613. The Americans could only take second place, scoring 94 medals against the East Germans' 90. The American President was so concerned about his country's performance that he ordered a special enquiry.

1976 Montreal: Juantorena, new style, new double

The Montreal games opened to the usual political storms. Black Africa marched out of the Olympics because of the presence of New Zealand, the nation with Rugby links with South Africa. Taiwanese competitors were stopped at the Canadian border in deference to Canada's links with China. The international unity of sport was once more shown to be a sham.

Yet, after the opening ceremony, the Cuban Juantorena went a long way towards giving Montreal something good to remember.

Sprint or middle distance?

It takes a very special athlete to double up over 400 and 800 metres. The 400m is still essentially in the domain of the sprinter. The 800m falls into the first category of middle distance running. This takes the two spheres of running into separate disciplines. Yet the gangling Alberto Juantorena mastered both techniques to achieve a unique double.

In the 400m heats he showed that nobody in Montreal was capable of living with him. He stood 6ft 3ins tall, had big thighs and an ungainly loping style. Yet the speed of the man was amazing.

He was the favourite for the 400m. But first he had to negotiate the longer distance and the big question was, could he do well in the 800m and still have sufficient left for the 400m? The answer was yes.

Ambling in the heats

Juantorena ambled through the heats and in the final faced a good, though not outstanding field. Ivo van Damme of Belgium, Dick Wohlhuter (USA), and the Yugoslav Luciano Susanj were good performers but not remarkable. The powerful Cuban proved himself a talent apart by outclassing the field and breaking the world record. He reached the bell in around 50 seconds and then shot away from the rest to clock 1min 43.5sec with van Damme second and Wohlhuter third.

After three 800m races and three prelims in the 400m, Juantorena saw the American, Fred Newhouse, three metres ahead in the 400m final. Then the giant Cuban began to run. He surged past his challenger to win in 44.26sec and become the first non-American to win the title since 1948.

Juantorena of Cuba managed to combine the skills of sprinting for the 400m with the skills of middle distance running for the 800m. The 400m was his event, but the 800m came first. Would he have the resources for both?

He won the 800m ahead of van Damme (Belgium) and Wohlhutter (USA).

The 400m – Juantorena ahead of Newhouse (USA)

1976 Montreal: Viren — flying by transfusion?

In 1972 Lasse Viren won both the 5,000 and 10,000 metres. In the four years since then he had done nothing. But now the arctic circle policeman, successor to Paavo Nurmi, beloved god of the Finns, was intent on defending his titles.

Only three other men had done the five and ten double before Viren — Kolehmainen (1912), Zatopek (1952) and Kuts (1956). None had achieved the double-double, both races in two successive Olympics.

Six out of six?

History, of course, now records that Viren realised the impossible dream. He won both titles in 1976 and is now busily engaged in his preparations for Moscow. Can he make it six out of six? Time will tell.

Lasse Viren (Finland) who has always denied suggestions that he used blood transfusions to boost the oxygen content of his body, won the 5,000m beating New Zealanders Quax and Dixon, and the 10,000m beating Lopez (Portugal) and Foster (GB).

The sprint medals went to the Caribbean, with Crawford winning the 100m and Quarrie the 200m.

What has never been revealed is the answer to the question, Did Viren undergo blood transfusions to boost the oxygen content of his body?' Finnish authorities have always rigorously denied the claim. But people close to athletics in Scandinavia categorically affirm their belief that he did.

In the event, he mastered the 10,000 metres field with an authority that left his rivals gasping. Britain's Brendan Foster was expected to give the modern Flying Finn a run for his money. But stricken by severe stomach upsets the Geordie had no response when Viren started his flight. Foster was overtaken for the silver by the Portuguese Carlos Lopez.

It was a different story in the 5,000m in which Dick Quax of New Zealand was beaten only fractionally by the Finn, and for most of the race Quax seemed more intent on beating his countryman Rod Dixon. It is possible that Quax did not realise the gold was within his grasp.

Caribbean challenge

Another popular double came in the sprints where the West Indians Haseley Crawford (100m gold) and Don Quarrie (200m gold) revived memories of Wint and McKenley with running and victories that once again illustrate the enormous talent Caribbean Islanders possess in the field of sport.

1976 Montreal: All speed, no effort

Every so often a runner flits across the Olympic skies like a shooting star, moving at great speed apparently without effort. The graceful style of Olympians like Herb Elliott, Bob Hayes, Kip Keino and Abebe Bikila live in the memory as much for their apparent effortlessness as their record-breaking abilities.

Moses rushes for gold

In Montreal, the natural successor to the speed-at-ease crown was the American 400m hurdler, Ed Moses. He took up this punishing race just four months before the games, yet he vanquished the opposition in spectacular style. Since then he has continued to dominate his event and is a hot favourite for Moscow.

In Montreal he used only 13 strides between the obstacles, flew along the flat with controlled power and hurdled with a minimum of movement. Moses seemed to flow and glide. He is easily the finest low hurdler ever seen.

He finished more than one second ahead of his team-mate, Mike Shine, with the Russian, Evgeniy Gavrilenko way back in third spot. Moses achieved the athletes double of gold combined with a world record time. He clocked 47.64sec and four years later it seems that there is no one capable of touching him.

Prophesy fulfilled

In the 110m hurdles it was an experienced campaigner who finally tasted success, Guy Drut of France. His victory fulfilled an amazing prophesy he made in 1975. He told the world he would win the Olympic title in 13.28sec. And so it was — right down to the last hundredth of a second.

Two men chased him hard, the Cuban Alejandro Casanas and America's Willie Davenport, who had won the title in 1968 and who had made his Olympic debut in 1964. The Cuban took the silver and Davenport the bronze. But there was no doubting Drut's command of the race.

The steeplechase was also dominated by one man, Anders Garderud of Sweden. Like Moses he hurdled without strain and flowed along the track like an unstoppable tide to sweep home in a world record time of 8mins 8.02sec. Just behind was the half-Scottish, Bronislaw Malinowski, from Poland.

Ed Moses (USA) took up hurdling only four months before the Olympics. Yet his perfect style – 13 strides between each obstacle – gave him easy victory in the 400m.

Guy Drut (France) foretold his 110m hurdles winning time to the last 100th of a second.

Anders Garderud (Sweden) also hurdled brilliantly to win the steeplechase.

1976 Montreal: Playing to the crowd is not enough

Very rarely does a man have the opportunity of avenging an Olympic defeat, but in 1976 Arnie Robinson had that satisfaction in the long jump pit. Four years previously he had seen form turned upside down by Randy Williams (USA). But this time Robinson made no mistakes.

His run-up had let him down at Munich, where he had to be satisfied with a bronze medal. Now he surged down the runway like a sprinter, soared into the air, and made a winning leap of 8m 35cm, nine inches better than Williams. Frank Wartenburg of East Germany finished third, and the Yugoslav, Nenad Stekic, who held the second best mark in the world after Bob Beamon's Mexico bound, could finish no better than fifth.

I love French Canadians

Dwight Stones, favourite for the high jump, went to Montreal and then left again, saying he wished to be in the United States for as long as possible, then fly in just to compete. The French Canadians took this as an insult to their facilities, an impression reinforced by Stones' criticism of the organisers.

In the preliminary rounds he was booed at every jump, and the police even heard of threats against him. So Stones then appeared with a T-shirt bearing the legend 'I love French Canadians'. It won the fans over, but did nothing to improve his jumping.

He finished third, outstayed by the Canadian, Greg Joy, who took the silver and by a young Pole, virtually unknown outside his own backyard. He was Jacek Wszola, then 19, who relished the rainy conditions and showed nerves of steel on the most important day of his life. He had failed at several early heights, while Joy had cleared them first time. So on a count back, the Canadian would have won. But young Wszola outstayed them all to take his prize at 2m 25cm.

Ironically, Stones went on to improve his own world record just four days later. But this was to be in fine weather and not in the slippery, cold atmosphere of Montreal that hindered his sharp run-up , more than that of the others.

Like father, like son

Every father wants his son to be a champion; more so if Dad has won a gold medal. Imre Nemeth (Hungary), won the hammer at the 1948 London games. In Montreal his son, Miklos, struck gold, with a javelin, thanks to a throw of 94m 58cm.

Nemeth hit a world record, as did the American, Bruce Jenner, who totalled 8,618pts in that most demanding event of them all, the decathlon.

Arnie Robinson (USA) avenged his 1972 defeat in the long jump.

Miklos Nemeth (Hungary) son of Imre Nemeth, who won the hammer gold in 1948, won the javelin.

Dwight Stones (USA) was unpopular with the crowds. He made efforts to please them, but could only manage a bronze medal.

1976 Montreal: African walk-out benefits New Zealand

At the 1974 Commonwealth Games in Christchurch, New Zealand, a young local lad, John Walker, surprised a lot of people by coming second to Filbert Bayi in the 1,500m. Bayi broke the world record that day as Walker was closing in on the Tanzanian.

The Africans had walked out of the Olympics because of the New Zealand rugby players. Ironically, this left the New Zealander, Walker, virtually without opposition at Montreal.

He had two options in the final: either he must make his own pace and run clear, or he must hang back and beat the field on the run-in. Either way he was better equipped than his rivals. He chose the second alternative. The race was run at a slow pace with Walker seventh after one lap and fourth after two.

A third lap of 58sec speeded things up and at the bell the Irishman, Eamonn Coghlan was shoulder to shoulder with Walker. Then, with memories of Jack Lovelock and Peter Snell, the famous All Black strip of New Zealand tore away from the field and Walker coasted home to an easy gold in 3mins 39.65sec.

Van Damme came in second, Paul Heinz Wellman (West Germany), third and Coghlan fourth. Van Damme was killed tragically a year later in a car accident in France.

Walker dominated the 1,500m and the East German, Cierpinski did likewise with the marathon.

At 25km Shorter (USA) broke away and only the German responded, to break away in his turn, 10km later, when Shorter couldn't respond again.

Dancing in a sombrero

East Germans finished second, third and fourth in the 20km walk, but the man who struck gold was Mexico's Daniel Bautista in 1hr 24mins 40.6sec. At the finish he dropped to his knees, crossed himself and kissed the ground, before dancing a lap of honour in a sombrero.

New Zealand's John Walker was the man to benefit from the absence of the Africans at Montreal. There was never much doubt that the 1,500m gold was his.

In the rainswept streets Cierpinski (East Germany) won the Marathon. Bautista (Mexico) won the 20km walk and then danced a lap of honour in a sombrero.

1976 Montreal: Hurricane girls from the east

At Tokyo in 1964 a young multi-lingual Polish girl, Irena Kirzenstein, won the silver medal in the long jump. She switched to running, married, had a baby and after three successful Olympics and four European Championships, here she was at Montreal still striking gold.

Medals in four games

Irena Szewinska, aged 30, won the 200m in Munich and was still one of the world's best sprinters. Wisely she concentrated all her efforts into the 400m in Montreal. She totally destroyed her rivals and her own world record by winning the final in 49.29sec — half a second faster than her previous mark. The second girl, Christina Brehmer of East Germany, was 10 metres away.

The Polish housewife had cruised in third and fourth in the prelims, but in the semi-final she showed that she was far from finished with a fine win. She thus made history by becoming the first woman athlete to win medals at four successive games.

Tatyana Kazankina went home to Russia with two gold medals after six punishing races — three over 800m and three over 1,500m. This wonder-girl was the centre of attraction in the 800m in which the first four girls all beat the previous world record. But Tatyana was well ahead in 1min 54.94sec. Twenty-four hours later she was off again in the heats for the 1,500m. Nothing seemed to bother her and in the final she outsprinted the East Germans Hoffmeister and Klapezynski.

Ruth is getting better

Another East German girl was not to be beaten so easily. Ruth Fuchs was the world record-holder and a javelin thrower extraordinary. Even in awful conditions of wind and rain she hurled the missile 65m 94cm, one-and-a-quarter metres further than the next girl. And Ruth will take some stopping in Moscow, for if anything, she is now throwing better than ever.

Angela Voigt took the long jump gold home to East Germany, with her first leap of 6m 72cm, and Rosi Ackerman won the high jump for East Germany at 1m 93cm from the Italian Sara Simeoni, who was 2cm behind. The Eastern bloc girls were a force to be reckoned with in Montreal.

Irena Szewinska (Poland) has won medals at four successive games.

Ruth Fuchs (East Germany) swept aside all opposition in the javelin. She is favourite for the event in Moscow.

Tatyana Kazankina (USSR) took home gold medals for the 800m and the 1,500m, after six races.

1976 Montreal: Wilkie alone against the USA

Although the games were almost in their own backyard, the American swimmers had one of their poorest ever Olympic returns. They won 34 of the 78 medals (43 per cent of the total) which was well down on their previous performances. Nonetheless, they won half the gold medals and all the men's events save one.

That one gold went to the Scot, David Wilkie, who had gone to an American University to get the kind of training and opposition he required for his Olympic build-up.

Breaking the barrier

Jim Montgomery and John Naber were to win seven golds between them, and Montgomery captured the public imagination in the 100m freestyle by crashing through the 50sec barrier — half a century after man had cracked the minute barrier! His winning time was 49.99sec. Montgomery went on to win two golds in the relays and a bronze in the 200m.

Naber won both backstroke events. The 100m saw the eclipse of the fabulous East German, Roland Matthes, who only took the bronze and then blew up in the opening round of the 200m backstroke.

Miami versus Stanford

The breaststroke was a battle between two men, Wilkie from Britain, via Miami University, and John Hencken who was at Stanford. Their rivalry dated back to Munich and neither was going to give way without a fight. Hencken was much shorter than Wilkie and faster over the 100m. Wilkie was firm favourite for the 200m. But everyone realised that there was little between the rivals.

Form worked out with Hencken breaking the world record in the heats and then reducing it further to 63.11sec in the final. Wilkie took silver in 63.43sec. Psychologically it was a good win for the American. Could he repeat it in the longer race?

Hencken well beaten

Whereas Wilkie had made a race of the 100m, Hencken was well beaten over 200m. Wilkie surged away from them all in a world record 2mins 15.11sec with his rival more than a body-length away. This one defeat scarcely dented the team morale of the Americans, who out-performed the East Germans and Australians.

American triple in the 200m freestyle.

The US swimming team's high morale, inspired by champions like Naber, who won two backstroke golds and came second to Furniss (USA) in the 200m freestyle, helped them to take all but one of the men's events.

The solitary non-American victory belonged to Wilkie (GB) in the 200m breaststroke. His bitter rival, Hencken, won the 100m, but came second in the 200m.

1976 Montreal: No opposition to the East Germans

Kornelia Ender dominated the women's swimming events with her powerful shoulders, and her rippling arm and leg muscles. She won the 100m and 200m in world record times; she was fractionally outside the minute barrier in the 100m butterfly (for another world record); she anchored the East German medley relay team to another gold medal in world record time. The 17 year-old schoolgirl from Bittefeld was indeed unstoppable. And only in the sprint relay did she fail to take gold.

Surprising first relay leg

The German coach surprisingly put her on the first leg against the American Kim Peyton. A surging finale by Shirley Babashoff gave the Americans victory. Shirley at last had a gold medal having had to accept three silvers behind the East Germans. There was no denying Miss Babashoff her moment of emotion — she laughed and wept at the same time.

In addition to Miss Ender, the East Germans had Petra Thumer who beat Babashoff into second place in both the 400m and the 800m. There was Ulrike Richter who won both backstroke events; Hannelore Anke (100m breast stroke); Andrea Pollack (200m butterfly); Ulrike Tauber (400m individual medley). Champions all, and part of the finest women's swimming team ever seen at the Olympics.

Not even the Russians got a look-in. Only in their traditional swimming event — the 200m breaststroke — did three Soviet girls manage to break the East German's stranglehold in the pool. Lined up in the final were three Russians, three East Germans and two British girls, Margaret Kelly and Debbie Rudd. Against such opposition they were destined only to follow.

It was not a fast race but the three Russians powered to the front early on and the aptly named Marina Kochevaia, Marina Yourtchenia and Liubov Rusanova ended up on the victory stand with three Red Flags being raised in salute. It made a welcome change — even for a western audience!

Kornelia Ender was only one of the most powerful women's swimming team seen at the Olympics. Thumer, Richter, Anke, Pollack and Tauber all won golds for East Germany.

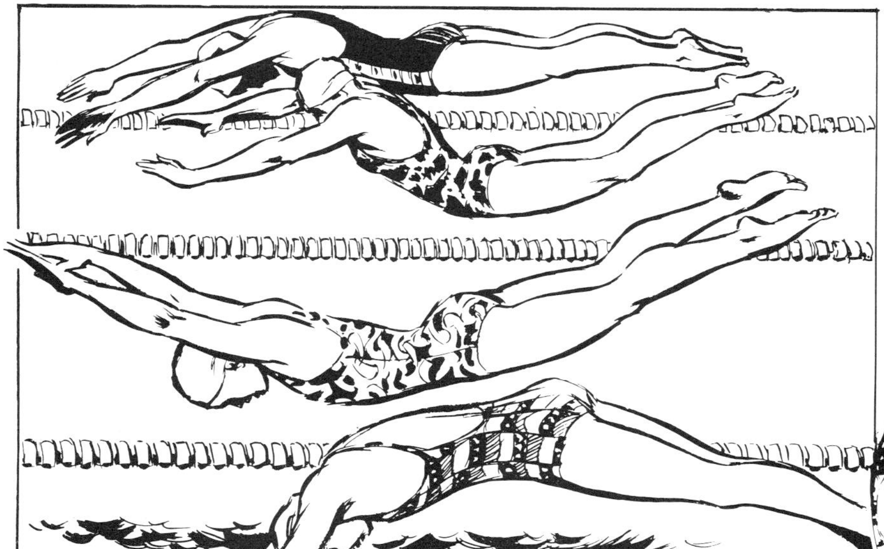

Kornelia Ender won gold medals in the 100m and 200m freestyle, the 100m butterfly and the medley relay, all in world record times.

1976 Montreal: Nadia, unsmiling, perfect, dedicated

As usual, competitors from the Orient and East Europe dominated the gymnastics. Standing above all was the little Rumanian pixie, Nadia Comaneci, who was only 14 but managed to sway the fans in the same way that Olga Korbut had done four years earlier in Munich.

Miss Comaneci scaled that enormous gymnastic mountain which brings ten points. She did it not once but seven times!

This most memorable figure — complete with plaits — won the combined gold medal, the asymetrical bars and the beam. For good measure she also took the bronze medal in the floor exercises. The unsmiling, dedicated girl allowed herself the luxury of a smile only after the points had been announced.

What a marked contrast to the beautiful and smiling Russian, Nelli Kim, who was a much more mature gymnast. She combined charm, appreciation and skill into a wonderful blend that placed her second to Comaneci overall and brought her the gold medals in the vault and floor exercises.

Russians challenge Japan

The Russians made a come-back in the men's competition with Nikolai Adrianov winning the combined exercises, the floor, the rings and the long horse contests. He also won a bronze in the pommel horse and a silver in the parallel bars. A good haul and the first serious challenger to the Japanese supremacy for a long time.

But this one-man show wasn't sufficient to prevent the Japanese taking the team prize, thanks largely to the way 29 year-old Sawao Kato held the team together with his brilliance and experienced leadership.

The Japanese did well to win the team event because their top man — Sigeru Kasamatsu — the world champion — missed the games through illness.

The calculated brilliance of Nadia Comaneci was the sensation of the Montreal gymnastics. She scored ten out of ten, seven times.

Nelli Kim, the charming Russian gymnast, was the only serious challenger to Rumania's Comaneci. The stars of the past, Tourischeva (USSR) and Korbut (USSR), had to be content with minor placings.

1976 Montreal: Disappointed riders and sailors

The horsemen and women of Britain usually do well at Olympic level, but they were way off course in Canada. In fact, for the first time since 1936 they won no medals.

Everything that could go wrong did so. The hastily organised dressage team had little hope of success. But the three day eventers were expected to do well, especially as Britain had won the team title in both Mexico and Munich.

Princess unseated

Even here things went badly right from the start. Princess Anne found *Goodwill* in temperamental form in the dressage and valuable points were lost. Then, at fence 19 on the cross-country course, she fell. Princess Anne finished 24th in the competition. Only Richard Meade, who finished fourth but well behind the bronze medal winner, did acceptably well.

Reg not Rodney

With horses and athletes out of form and most British swimmers apparently in danger of drowning, hopes rested largely on the shoulders of the sailors. But here succes was hard come by, save in the *Tornado* class where Reg White was supreme.

He won four of his six races and took fourth and fifth positions in the other two. He won with 18 points, half the total of the second man, the American McFaul.

It seemed that Rodney Pattisson would again win the *Flying Dutchman* class, but a disasterous fifth race, in which he finished 18th, put him out of contention and into the silver medal slot.

Unexpected gold

A gold did come for Britain in a most unexpected quarter — the modern pentathlon. This event comprises riding, fencing, shooting, swimming and cross country running.

The British trio of Sergeant Jim Fox, Adrian Parker and Danny Nightingale did well in the riding and swimming, but their strongest event was still to come, the lung-sapping cross-country. Fox said before the race they were in with a chance of the bronze. But after Parker had clocked 12mins 9sec in the first run of the day, the British were way out ahead. Nightingale was only 20sec slower on his run, and then Fox ran himself to a standstill in 12mins 47sec and collapsed into the arms of two Canadian soldiers at the end of the race. And the prize was theirs — much to many people's astonishment.

Reg White (GB) won the Tornado catamaran sailing convincingly. But Pattisson (GB) failed to repeat his Flying Dutchman wins of 1968 and 1972.

British riding hopes were high, but Princess Anne on Goodwill could only manage 24th position, having failed in the cross country. Meade came fourth.

Records and results: 1976

The war in the water

American men and the East German women swept all competition aside in Munich. In the men's events the US team took 12 out of 13 events. Britain's David Wilkie prevented a US whitewash. In the women's events the East Germans took 11 out of 13 gold medals. East Germany had never won a women's swimming event before.

Men's swimming

100m freestyle	Jim Montgomery (USA)	49.99sec, world record
200m freestyle	Bruce Furniss (USA)	1min 50.29sec, world record
400m freestyle	Brian Goodell (USA)	3mins 51.93sec, world record
1,500m freestyle	Brian Goodell (USA)	15mins 02.4sec, world record
100m backstroke	John Naber (USA)	55.49sec, world record
200m backstroke	John Naber (USA)	1min 59.19sec, world record
100m breaststroke	John Hencken (USA)	1min 03.11sec, world record
200m breaststroke	David Wilkie (GB)	2mins 15.11sec, world record
100m butterfly	Matt Vogel (USA)	54.35sec
200m butterfly	Mike Bruner (USA)	1min 59.23sec, world record
400m medley	Rod Strachan (USA)	4mins 23.68sec, world record
4 x 200m freestyle relay	USA	7mins 23.27sec, world record
4 x 100m medley relay	USA	3mins 42.22sec, world record

Women's swimming

100m freestyle	Kornelia Ender (East Germany)	55.65sec, world record
200m freestyle	Kornelia Ender (East Germany)	1min 59.26sec, world record
400m freestyle	Petra Thumer (East Germany)	4mins 09.89sec, world record
800m freestyle	Petra Thumer (East Germany)	8mins 37.14sec, world record
100m breaststroke	Hannelore Anke (East Germany)	1min 11.16sec, Olympic record
200m breaststroke	Marina Koshevaya (USSR)	2mins 33.35sec, world record
100m butterfly	Kornelia Ender (East Germany)	1min 00.13sec, world record
200m butterfly	Andrea Pollack (East Germany)	2mins 11.41sec Olympic record
100m backstroke	Ulrike Richter (East Germany)	1min 01.83sec Olympic record
200m backstroke	Ulrike Richter (East Germany)	2mins 13.43sec Olympic record
400m individual medley	Ulrike Tauber (East Germany)	4mins 42.77sec, world record
4 x 100m freestyle relay	USA	3mins 44.82sec, world record
4 x 100m medley relay	East Germany	4mins 07.95sec, world record

The Cuban Colossus

Alberto Juantorena was the first runner to win gold in both 400m and 800m. Here is how he did it:

400m

Round one, heat six:	1. A. Juantorena (47.89sec)
Round two, heat two:	2. A. Juantorena (45.92sec)
Semi-final:	1. A. Juantorena (45.1sec)
Final:	1. A. Juantorena (44.26sec)
	2. F. Newhouse (USA) (44.4sec)
	3. H. Frazier (USA) (44.95sec)

800m

Round one, heat four:	1. A. Juantorena (1min 47.15sec)
Semi-final:	1. A. Juantorena (1min 45.88sec)
Final:	1. A. Juantorena (1min 43.5sec), new world record
	2. I. van Damme (Belgium) (1min 43.86sec)
	3. R. Wohlhuter (USA) (1min 44.12sec)

Viren's double double

Lasse Viren of Finland has achieved the amazing feat of winning both the 5,000m and the 10,000m in two games. Here are his results:

1972 Munich

5,000m Final
1. Viren (Finland) 13mins 26.4sec
2. Gammoudi (Tunisia) 13mins 27.4sec
3. Stewart (GB) 13mins 27 6sec

10,000m Final
1. Viren (Finland) 27mins 38.4sec
2. Puttemans (Belgium) 27mins 39.6sec
3. Yifter (Ethiopia) 27mins 41sec

1976 Montreal

5,000m Final
1. Viren (Finland) 13mins 24.76sec
2. Quax (New Zealand) 13mins 25.15sec
3. Hildenbrand (West Germany) 13mins 25.38sec

10,000m Final
1. Viren (Finland) 27mins 40.38sec
2. Lopes (Portugal) 27mins 45.17sec
3. Foster (GB) 27mins 54.92sec

Fighting for Fidel

Teofilo Stevenson (Cuba) won the heavyweight boxing in both the Munich and Montreal games. In Moscow he will defend his title. So far none of his Olympic opponents has gone three full rounds with him.

1972

Stevenson v L. Denderys (Poland): stopped in round one.
Stevenson v D. Bobick (USA): stopped in round three.
Stevenson v P. Hussing (West Germany): stopped in round two.
Final:
Stevenson v I. Alexe (Rumania): walkover, Alexe injured.

1976

Stevenson v M. Drame (Senegal): knockout in round two.
Stevenson v P. Ruskola (Finland): stopped in round one.
Stevenson v J. Tate (USA) knockout in round one.
Final:
Stevenson v M. Simon (Rumania): stopped in round three.

1980 Moscow: Two middle distance hopes

Track and field events are the core of the Olympics. Yet, curiously, no host nation has managed to dominate competition at the main stadium since the war.

In 1956 the Australian girls did well at Melbourne. But this apart, the post-war games have been a frustrating experience for home team supporters.

Moscow citizens seem to be in for the same treatment. The rise of East Germany has coincided with a falling off of standards in the Soviet Union.

Blue riband event

In the English-speaking world the 1,500m, the metric mile, is still the blue riband event of all track competitions. And for once British hopes of success are both high and realistic. We possess not one, but two contenders if 1979 form is maintained.

Sebastian Coe, who smashed world marks over 800m and 1,500m and the mile in that spectacular 41 day spree last summer, and Steve Ovett are the favourites in most people's minds.

Sebastian Coe (GB)

Steve Ovett (GB)

John Walker (NZ)

Bayi and Walker past their best

Since winning his gold in 1976, the New Zealander John Walker has suffered a series of operations on both legs and cannot be as powerful as before. The 1974 Commonwealth 1,500m champion, Filbert Bayi of Tanzania, probably lost his chance for good when the Africans walked out of Montreal.

The last middle-distance gold medal won by a Briton was way back in 1932 when Tommy Hampson won the 800m in Los Angeles. But surely this time the medal drought can be ended.

Coe the main hope

The British selectors see Coe as our main hope for the 800m, with Ovett the top contender in the longer race. Coe has certainly shown his more impressive form over two laps, but he has only run six 1,500m or mile races — and in two of them he broke good world records. Neither race was a soft touch. With another year's stamina training behind him he could be the man to beat in the 1,500m.

Juantorena's defence

Certainly the giant Cuban, Alberto Juantorena, will be there to defend his 400m and 800m titles. His superior strength might yet prove the decisive factor in a tight finish with the less robust Coe.

In realistic terms Coe and Ovett are the only British competitors capable of striking gold in Moscow. But Daley Thompson must be in with a bronze medal chance at least in the decathlon. Also Tessa Sanderson is certainly a medal prospect in the women's javelin. Unluckily for Tessa, she's in the event dominated by the East German Amazon, Ruth Fuchs. And there are few hotter favourites for an Olympic title.

American pacemen in force

The Americans will be out in force in the sprints, having failed to win the 100m and 200m in the last two Olympics. Houston McTear, who comes from a poor family in the Everglades of Florida, is one of the hottest properties in world sprinting and the 100m is his main event.

Daley Thompson (GB)

McTear, as a 19 year-old, missed out on Montreal with a pulled muscle. But he was back to form in 1979.

Britain's Alan Wells has enjoyed three excellent seasons, picking off most of the top men one at a time. He showed in the Commonwealth Games in 1978 that he is a man for all venues with a gold and silver at Edmonton, Alberta. But the solid phalanx of American, Caribbean and East European talent makes it tough to tip him. But on his best day he has the ability — more so than Daley and Tessa — to upset all the odds and beat the best.

1980 Moscow: Famous faces back again

Lasse Viren (Finland)

Can Lasse Viren score a treble double? This intriguing question has to be asked because he has spent the last three years quietly preparing for the 5,000m and 10,000m just as he did in the three year period leading up to Montreal. To have achieved the double twice was an amazing performance but now age might have caught up with the Flying Finnish policeman.

Miruts Yifter of Ethiopia will take some catching over the longer distance. And Henry Rono of Kenya could be the man to dominate both the 5,000m and steeplechase. In fact, having missed Montreal, it could be the Africans who will score in Moscow.

Ruth Fuchs (E. Germany)

East German lionesses

In women's athletics the power of East Germany will undoubtedly build up their medals total. Only in the 1,500m and 3,000m are the Russian girls strong enough to make a serious track challenge.

There is one lone ranger — an ace in the pack — who could upset all the East German plans for gold medals in the sprints.

Evelyn Ashford (USA) had a spectacular season in 1979. Her performances over 100m were consistently outstanding throughout the summer. She has an explosive start, superb pick-up and a driving finish. Not since Wilma Rudolph in 1960 have the Americans produced a sprinter of such commanding capabilities.

Even the Renata Stechers of the East German production line will find it difficult to keep up with Evelyn. Her married name is Washington and this seems an additional omen for success at the Lenin Stadium.

Moses the king

The one competitor who stands head and shoulders above the rest in his event is Ed Moses, who will be defending his 400m hurdles title.

Ed Moses (USA)

Hurdlers (except Moses who learned in a few months) take years to learn their craft and there has been nobody on the horizon to challenge this mighty man in his speciality. His controlled power and fluency almost make the hurdles seem non-existent. He is the natural successor to David Hemery and John Akii-Bua in reducing the obstacles to minimal proportions.

Five Olympics for Szewinska

Irena Szewinska has won medals at the last four Olympics She is the Princess of Polish athletics who always raises her performance when it matters most. She must be in with a

Alberto Juantorena (Cuba)

chance. From a start in long jumping she has moved through the ranks of sprinting up to 400m. She will be defending this title in Moscow. But perhaps her main target this time will be the 800m. Another medal for her mantlepiece in Warsaw would be as popular as it would be unique.

Tributes to the heavyweight

Like Ed Moses in the 400m hurdles, one boxer of truly outstanding strength seems unbeatable. He is, of course, Teofilo Stevenson of Cuba who won the heavyweight gold in such style in Montreal. Stevenson could have walked into the professional arena after the last games and made himself a millionaire.

He was certainly a better gold medalist than Floyd Patterson and Joe Frazier. His performance is arguably as good as that of Cassius Clay in Rome in 1960. Clay — later to become Muhammad Ali — has paid great tributes to Stevenson and this itself speaks volumes for the Cuban's ability.

1980 Moscow: The Chinese factor

Nadia Comaneci (Rumania)

The nymph-like Nadia Comaneci will be 18 this time round and the darling of 1976 could find that the Russians have girls who will beat her this time. Much is still expected of Nelli Kim who has maintained her position as the top Soviet gymnast and natural successor to Korbut and Tourischeva. In the men's competition the Russian team will be on tip-toe to attain the highest quality, for they know the Japanese will be strong.

The gymnastics hall should be the place where Russian fans will have most to shout about. Throughout the years, failed ballet dancers in the Soviet Union have gone into gymnastics to utilise their gifts. It will be surprising if they fail in front of their own supporters.

The life of a swimmer these days is so short. Women competitors are regarded as old ladies at 17. Kornelia Ender, star of 1976 is married with a child. So predicting the new Olympic heroines is impossible more than a few weeks before the games. The young carefree Californians, with their sunny approach, won't be locked into their trials until mid-summer. But Cynthia Woodhead and Tracy Caulkins will probably be there for America. Bogdanora will probably uphold Russian traditions in the breaststroke.

East German production line

Two things are for sure. The American men will scoop the pool, and the American girls will be almost alone in mounting a concentrated challenge to the mighty East Germans, whose production line is relentlessly producing a new series of wonderswimmers to be shown to the world a month or two before Moscow.

The horses are the professionals

In equestrianism, where the big money prizes have been going to the horses for years, thus maintaining the amateur status of the riders, things have changed. Competitors like Harvey Smith and David Broome have become full time professionals.

So a new generation of horsemen and women will be on duty in 1980. Harvey's sons will follow him into the Olympics, if not at Moscow then at Los Angeles. Both are young with many years of competition ahead.

In the Gulf of Finland, off Tallin, the British sailors know that a strong team of Germans — from East and West — will be their main rivals. They also believe that the Russian sailors, with deep knowledge of their local waters, could be the surprise medallists in all classes.

The Chinese are back

But the biggest surprises of all could be provided by the re-appearing Chinese. They are back in the Olympic fold after an absence of three decades. In recent competitions, like the Asian Games, they have shown immense power in areas like high jumping, pistol and rifle shooting, gymnastics, volleyball, archery and fencing.

Teofilo Stevenson (Cuba)

The unknown factors are what makes sport the exciting attraction it is. And the unknown factor of China's presence will lend a new dimension to the 1980 Olympics.

In 1952 the large Russian team stole much of the glory at Helsinki.

Nelli Kim (USSR)

Nadia Comaneci (Rumania)

Throughout the 1960s and into the 1970s the African advance was the hallmark of the widening scope of the games. On now into the 1980s. Is this to be the sporting decade of China? Their opening, tentative steps in Moscow will give a broad clue to the answer to that question.

BERG

Your personal record of the 1980 Olympics

Fill in the results of the major competitions on these two pages. A complete list of events taking place in Moscow appears overleaf.

Athletics — men

100m ____
200m ____
400m ____
800m ____
1,500m ____
5,000m ____
10,000m ____
Marathon ____
110m hurdles ____
400m hurdles ____
3,000m steeplechase ____
20km walk ____
50km walk ____
4 x 100m relay ____
4 x 400m relay ____
High jump ____
Long jump ____
Triple jump ____
Pole vault ____
Shot ____
Discus ____
Hammer ____
Javelin ____
Decathlon ____

Athletics — women

100m ____
200m ____
400m ____
800m ____
1,500m ____
100m hurdles ____
4 x 100m relay ____
4 x 400m relay ____
High jump ____
Long jump ____
Shot ____
Discus ____
Javelin ____
Pentathlon ____

Basketball ____

Boxing

Light flyweight ____
Flyweight ____
Bantamweight ____
Featherweight ____
Lightweight ____
Light welterweight ____
Welterweight ____
Light middleweight ____
Middleweight ____
Light heavyweight ____
Heavyweight ____

Cycling

Ind pursuit ____
Team pursuit ____
1,000m sprint ____
1,000m time trial ____
Team time trial ____
Road race ____

Equestrian

Show jumping (Ind) ____
Show jumping (Team) ____
Dressage (Ind) ____
Dressage (Team) ____
Three day event (Ind) ____
Three day event (Team) ____

Football ____

Gymnastics — men

Combined exercises (Ind) ____
Combined exercises (Team) ____
Floor exercises ____
Horizontal bar ____
Parallel bars ____
Pommelled horse ____
Long horse vault ____
Rings ____

Gymnastics — women
Combined exercises (Ind) ____________
Combined exercises (Team) ____________
Beam ____________
Asymmetrical bars ____________
Horse vault ____________
Floor exercises ____________

Handball ____________

Hockey ____________

Modern pentathlon (Ind) ____________

Modern pentathlon (Team) ____________

Rowing — men
Single sculls ____________
Double sculls ____________
Coxless pairs ____________
Coxed pairs ____________
Coxless fours ____________
Coxed fours ____________
Eights ____________

Rowing — women
Single sculls ____________
Double sculls ____________
Coxless pairs ____________
Coxed pairs ____________
Eights ____________

Swimming — men
100m freestyle ____________
200m freestyle ____________
400m freestyle ____________
1,500m freestyle ____________
100m backstroke ____________
200m backstroke ____________
100m butterfly ____________
200m butterfly ____________
100m breaststroke ____________
200m breaststroke ____________
200m ind medley ____________
400m ind medley ____________
4 x 100m freestyle relay ____________
4 x 200m freestyle relay ____________
Springboard diving ____________
High diving ____________
Water polo ____________

Swimming — women
100m freestyle ____________
200m freestyle ____________
400m freestyle ____________
800m freestyle ____________
100m backstroke ____________
200m backstroke ____________
100m butterfly ____________
200m butterfly ____________
100m breaststroke ____________
200m breaststroke ____________
200m ind medley ____________
400m ind medley ____________
4 x 100m freestyle relay ____________
4 x 200m freestyle relay ____________
Springboard diving ____________
High diving ____________

Volleyball ____________

Weightlifting
Flyweight ____________
Bantamweight ____________
Featherweight ____________
Lightweight ____________
Middleweight ____________
Light Heavyweight ____________
Middle Heavyweight ____________
Heavyweight ____________
Super heavyweight ____________

Yachting
Tempest ____________
Finn ____________
Tornado ____________
Soling ____________
Flying Dutchman ____________
470 ____________

1980 Olympic programme

This is the list of events that will take place not only in the Soviet capital, but also in various other centres. The 1980 Olympic games begin on Saturday July 19 and end on Sunday August 3.

Event	JULY													AUGUST		
	19 Sat	20 Sun	21 Mon	22 Tues	23 Wed	24 Thur	25 Fri	26 Sat	27 Sun	28 Mon	29 Tues	30 Wed	31 Thur	1 Fri	2 Sat	3 Sun
Opening Ceremony	■															
Basketball		■	■	■	■		■	■	■	■		■				
Boxing		■	■	■	■	■	■	■	■	■	■	■	■		■	
Wrestling-Freestyle									■	■	■	■	■			
- Greco-Roman		■	■	■	■	■										
Judo									■	■	■	■	■	■	■	
Cycling Track				■	■	■	■	■								
Cycling Road		■								■						
Volleyball		■	■	■	■	■	■	■	■	■	■	■		■		
Gymnastics		■	■	■	■	■	■									
Rowing		■	■	■	■	■		■	■							
Canoeing												■	■	■	■	
Equestrian						■	■	■	■		■	■	■	■		■
Track and Field						■	■	■	■	■		■	■	■		
Yachting		■													■	
Swimming		■	■	■	■	■		■	■							
Diving		■	■	■	■		■	■	■	■						
Waterpolo		■	■	■		■	■	■		■	■					
Handball		■	■	■	■	■	■	■	■	■	■	■				
Modern Pentathlon		■	■	■	■	■										
Archery												■	■	■	■	
Shooting		■	■	■	■	■	■	■								
Weightlifting		■	■	■	■	■		■	■	■	■	■				
Fencing				■	■	■	■	■	■	■	■	■	■			
* Football		■	■	■	■	■	■		■		■			■	■	
Field Hockey		■	■		■	■	■	■	■	■	■	■	■	■		
Closing Ceremony																■

* In Minsk, Kiev and Leningrad, as well as Moscow

Programme chart courtesy of David Dryer (Sports Travel) Ltd.